T0091270

The Big Book of
Restorative Justice

Published titles include:

The Little Book of Restorative Justice: Revised & Updated,
by Howard Zehr

The Little Book of Conflict Transformation, by John Paul Lederach

The Little Book of Family Group Conferences, New-Zealand Style, by
Allan MacRae and Howard Zehr

The Little Book of Strategic Peacebuilding, by Lisa Schirch

The Little Book of Strategic Negotiation,
by Jayne Seminare Docherty

The Little Book of Circle Processes, by Kay Pranis

The Little Book of Contemplative Photography, by Howard Zehr

The Little Book of Restorative Discipline for Schools, by Lorraine
Stutzman Amstutz and Judy H. Mullet

The Little Book of Trauma Healing, by Carolyn Yoder

The Little Book of Biblical Justice, by Chris Marshall

The Little Book of Restorative Justice for People in Prison,
by Barb Toews

The Little Book of Cool Tools for Hot Topics,
by Ron Kraybill and Evelyn Wright

El Pequeño Libro de Justicia Restaurativa, by Howard Zehr

The Little Book of Dialogue for Difficult Subjects,
by Lisa Schirch and David Campt

The Little Book of Victim Offender Conferencing,
by Lorraine Stutzman Amstutz

The Little Book of Restorative Justice for Colleges and Universities, by
David R. Karp

The Little Book of Restorative Justice for Sexual Abuse, by Judah
Oudshoorn with Michelle Jackett and Lorraine Stutzman Amstutz

*The Big Book of Restorative Justice: Four Classic Justice &
Peacebuilding Books in One Volume,* by Howard Zehr, Lorraine
Stutzman Amstutz, Allan MacRae, and Kay Pranis

The Little Book of Transformative Community Conferencing,
by David Anderson Hooker

The Little Book of Restorative Justice in Education,
by Katherine Evans and Dorothy Vaandering

The Little Book of Restorative Justice for Older Adults,
by Julie Friesen and Wendy Meek

The Little Book of Race and Restorative Justice, by Fania E. Davis

The Little Book of Racial Healing,
by Thomas Norman DeWolf, Jodie Geddes

The Little Book of Restorative Teaching Tools,
by Lindsey Pointer, Kathleen McGoey, and Haley Farrar

The Little Book of Police Youth Dialogue
by Dr. Micah E. Johnson and Jeffrey Weisberg

The Little Book of Youth Engagement in Restorative Justice
by Evelín Aquino, Anita Wadhwa, and Heather Bligh Manchester

The Little Books of Justice & Peacebuilding present, in highly
accessible form, key concepts and practices from the fields of
restorative justice, conflict transformation, and peacebuilding. Written
by leaders in these fields, they are designed for practitioners, students,
and anyone interested in justice, peace, and conflict resolution.

The Little Books of Justice & Peacebuilding series is a cooperative
effort between the Center for Justice and Peacebuilding of Eastern
Mennonite University and publisher Good Books.

The Big Book of Restorative Justice

Four Classic Justice & Peacebuilding Books in One Volume

HOWARD ZEHR, LORRAINE S. AMSTUTZ, ALLAN MACRAE, AND KAY PRANIS

Good Books

New York, New York

Copyright © 2022 by Good Books, an imprint of Skyhorse Publishing, Inc.

All rights reserved. No part of this book may be reproduced in any manner without the express written consent of the publisher, except in the case of brief excerpts in critical reviews or articles. All inquiries should be addressed to Good Books, 307 West 36th Street, 11th Floor, New York, NY 10018.

Good Books books may be purchased in bulk at special discounts for sales promotion, corporate gifts, fund-raising, or educational purposes. Special editions can also be created to specifications. For details, contact the Special Sales Department, Good Books, 307 West 36th Street, 11th Floor, New York, NY 10018 or info@skyhorsepublishing.com.

Good Books is an imprint of Skyhorse Publishing, Inc.®, a Delaware corporation.

Visit our website at www.goodbooks.com.

10 9 8 7 6 5 4 3 2 1

Library of Congress Cataloging-in-Publication Data is available on file.

Print ISBN: 978-1-68099-763-7
eBook ISBN: 978-1-68099-798-9

Printed in the United States of America

The Justice & Peacebuilding series presents, in highly accessible form, key concepts and practices from the fields of restorative justice, conflict transformation, and peacebuilding. Written by leaders in these fields, they are designed for practitioners, students, and anyone interested in justice, peace, and conflict resolution.

The Justice & Peacebuilding series is a cooperative effort between the Center for Justice and Peacebuilding of Eastern Mennonite University and publisher Good Books.

Contents

Foreword

I began the Little Books of Justice and Peacebuilding series to introduce and summarize core concepts and practices in a concise, readable, and inexpensive format—little books that you can read quickly, carry easily, and afford to give away or use in a class or discussion group.

But maybe you want the core books of restorative justice compiled into one volume so that you can read them and keep them together. Maybe you want to have a text for a class you are teaching or taking. If so, this *Big Book* is for you.

The field of restorative justice has grown exponentially since these books were initially released, expanding into new areas of application. Nevertheless, the four books included here continue to provide a solid grounding in the philosophy and values of restorative justice as well as basic models of practice.

The models of practice described in this book—victim offender conferencing, family group conferencing, circle processes—are methodologies that are being implemented in many arenas and many places. However, they are not "cookie-cutters" to be simply copied and implemented; at minimum, they must be adapted to the context. At best, they provide suggestions and inspiration. It has been gratifying to see, for example, how the model of family group conference from New Zealand has been adapted and implemented in creative ways in other parts of the world.

But restorative justice is much more than specific models of practice. It is more than even the best circle practices. Most fundamental is the concept or philosophy of restorative justice—the principles and values that undergird and guide it. Using these principles and values as a guide, restorative justice can be applied to many situations, regardless of whether practice models are in place. Without these principles and values, restorative justice is very likely to be misused and to go astray, that is, to become something that was not intended.

As I note in the first book in this volume, some have called restorative justice a philosophy of life, a way of living together that, in the face of the divisive, individualizing forces of modern society, reminds us that we are connected to one another. Restorative justice is about building and maintaining healthy relationships and repairing them when they are damaged.

The volumes bound together in this *Big Book of Restorative Justice* suggest important values and guidelines for the difficult times in which we live.

—Howard Zehr

THE LITTLE BOOK OF
Restorative Justice

Revised and Updated

HOWARD ZEHR

Table of Contents

Acknowledgments

Aspecial thanks to the many friends and colleagues who gave me feedback on this manuscript. This includes my students, former students, and colleagues at the Center for Justice and Peacebuilding where I have taught since 1996. I especially want to thank Barb Toews, Jarem Sawatsky, Bonnie Price Lofton, Robert Gillette, Vernon Jantzi, Larissa Fast, and Ali Gohar for their careful attention and suggestions.

For this new edition, I am especially thankful to Sujatha Baliga for her careful reading and suggestions.

CHAPTER 1

An Overview

How should we as a society respond to wrongdoing? When a crime occurs, when an injustice or harm is committed, what needs to happen? What does justice require? The urgency of this question is emphasized daily by events reported in the media.

Whether we are concerned with crime or other offenses and harms, the Western legal system has profoundly shaped our thinking about these issues—not only in the Western world, but in much of the rest of the world as well.

The Western legal system's approach to justice has some important strengths. Yet there is also a growing acknowledgment of this system's limits and failures. Those who have been harmed, those who have caused harm, and

---

community members in general often feel that the criminal justice process shaped by this legal system does not adequately meet their needs. Justice professionals—law enforcement officers, judges, lawyers, prosecutors, probation and parole officers, prison staff—frequently express a sense of frustration as well. Many feel that the criminal justice process deepens societal wounds and conflicts rather than contributing to healing or peace.

Restorative justice is an attempt to address some of these needs and limitations. Since the 1970s, a variety of programs and practices have emerged in thousands of communities and many countries throughout the world. Often these are offered as choices within or alongside the existing legal system, although in some occasions they are used as an alternative to the existing system. Since 1989, New Zealand has made restorative conferences the hub of its entire youth justice system.

In many places today, restorative justice is considered a sign of hope and the direction of the future. Whether it will live up to this promise remains to be seen, but many are optimistic.

Restorative justice began as an effort to deal with burglary and other property crimes that are usually viewed (often incorrectly) as relatively minor offenses. Today, however, restorative approaches are available in some communities for the most severe forms of criminal violence: death from drunken driving, assault, rape, even murder. Building upon the experience of the Truth and Reconciliation Commission in South Africa, efforts are also being made to apply a restorative justice framework to situations of mass violence.

These approaches and practices are also spreading beyond the criminal justice system to schools and universities, to the workplace, and to religious institutions. Some advocate the use of restorative approaches such as circles processes (a practice that emerged from First Nation communities in Canada) as a way to work through, resolve, and transform conflicts in general. Others pursue circle processes and other restorative approaches as a way to build and heal communities. Kay Pranis, a prominent restorative justice advocate, calls circles a form of participatory democracy that moves beyond simple majority rule.

In societies where Western legal systems have replaced and/or suppressed traditional justice and conflict-resolution processes, restorative justice is providing a framework to reexamine and sometimes reactivate these traditions. I sometimes envision restorative justice as a blend of key elements in modern human rights sensibilities and traditional approaches to harm or conflict.

Although the term "restorative justice" encompasses a variety of programs and practices, at its core it is a set of principles and values, a philosophy, an alternate set of guiding questions. Ultimately, restorative justice provides an alternative framework for thinking about wrongdoing. I will explore that framework in the pages that follow and illustrate how it translates into practice.

Why this *Little Book*?

In this *Little Book*, my intention is not to make the case for restorative justice. Nor do I explore the many implications of this approach. Rather, I intend this book to be a brief description or overview—the *CliffsNotes*, if you will—of restorative justice. Although I will outline some of the programs and practices of restorative justice, my focus in this book is especially the principles or philosophy of restorative justice. Other books in this *Little Books of Justice & Peacebuilding* series explore practice models more thoroughly; a list of these is provided at the end of this book.

The Little Book of Restorative Justice is for those who have heard the term and are curious about what it implies. But it is also an attempt to bring clarity to those of us involved in the field because it is so easy to lose clarity about our direction and what we have set out to do.

All social innovations have a tendency to lose their way as they develop and spread, and restorative justice is no different. With more and more programs being termed "restorative justice," the meaning of that phrase is sometimes diluted or confused. Under the inevitable pressures of working in the real world, restorative justice has sometimes been subtly coopted or diverted from its principles.

> **Restorative justice claims to be victim-oriented.**

The victim advocacy community has been especially concerned about this. Restorative justice claims to be victim-oriented, but is it really? All too often, victim groups fear, restorative justice efforts have been motivated mainly by a desire to work with those who have offended in a more positive way. Like the criminal system that it aims to improve or replace, restorative justice may become primarily a way to deal with those who have offended.

Others wonder whether the field has adequately addressed the needs of those who have offended and made sufficient efforts to help them become their best selves. Do restorative justice programs give adequate support to those who have caused harm to carry out their obligations and to change their patterns of behavior? Do restorative justice programs adequately address the harms that may have led those who cause harm to become who they are? Are such programs becoming just another way to punish those who have harmed under a new guise? And what about the community at large? Is the community being adequately both allowed and encouraged to be involved and to assume its obligations?

Another concern is whether in articulating and practicing restorative justice, we are replicating patterns of racial and economic disparities that are prevalent in society. Is restorative justice as practiced in the United States, for example, being applied primarily for white folks? Is it adequately addressing underlying disparities?

Our past experience with change efforts in the justice arena warns us that sidetracks and diversions from our visions and models inevitably happen in spite of our best intentions. If advocates for change are unwilling to acknowledge and address these likely diversions, their efforts may end up much different than they intended. In fact, "improvements" can turn out to be worse than the conditions that they were designed to reform or replace.

One of the most important safeguards we can exert against such sidetracks is to give attention to core principles and values. If we are clear about principles and values, if we design our programs with these in mind, if we are open to being evaluated by these principles and values, we are much more likely to stay on track.

Put another way, the field of restorative justice has grown so rapidly and in so many directions that it is sometimes difficult to know how to move into the future with integrity and creativity. Only a clear vision of principles and goals can provide the compass we need as we find our way along a path that is inevitably winding and unclear.

This book is an effort to articulate the restorative justice concept and its principles in straightforward terms. However, I must acknowledge certain limits to the framework I will lay out here. Even though I have tried hard to remain critical and open, I come with a bias in favor of this ideal. Moreover, in spite of all efforts to the contrary, I write from my own "lens," and that is shaped by who I am: a white, middle-class male of European ancestry, a Christian, a Mennonite. This biography and these, as well as other, interests and values necessarily shape my voice and vision.

Even though there is somewhat of a consensus within the field about the broad outline of the principles of restorative justice, not all that follows is uncontested. What you read here is my understanding of restorative justice. It must be tested against the voices of others.

Finally, I've written this book within a North American context. The terminology, the issues raised, and even the way the concept is formulated reflect to some extent the realities of my setting. The first edition has been widely translated into other languages, but the translations needed for other contexts go beyond language.

With this background and these qualifications, then, what is "restorative justice"? So many misconceptions have grown up around the term that I find it increasingly important to first clarify what, in my view, restorative justice is *not*. Before I do that, however, I'll make a few comments about this revised edition.

About this revised edition

Much has happened since this book was first released in 2002. The book itself has sold more than 110,000 copies and has been translated and released in countries as disparate as Japan, the former Czechoslovakia, Pakistan, and Iran. As this suggests, the restorative justice field has continued to spread and develop over these years, and well beyond the criminal justice context. In fact, cities in the United Kingdom, New Zealand, South Korea, and elsewhere have been exploring what it means to become restorative cities. A few health care systems in the U.S. have adopted restoratively-oriented approaches to address cases of possible medical malpractice, allowing patients and doctors to interact much more freely in meeting needs and addressing obligations. Some advocates have argued that restorative justice is, in fact, a way of life.

Within the United States, at least, perhaps the biggest growth area for restorative justice has been in schools and, more recently, in the area of university conduct. This book tends to have a criminal justice focus, but several books in this *Little Books* series now address these educational contexts specifically.

Expansion has occurred within the criminal justice arena. The majority of U.S. states now have some reference to restorative justice principles or practices within their statutes and policies. Several countries have developed nation-wide models inspired by restorative justice. At the time of the first edition, most applications for using restorative justice for criminal cases came after there were formal charges. However, applications to keep cases out of the formal system, sometimes in an effort to address racial disparities, are now becoming more frequent.

Michelle Alexander's important book, *The New Jim Crow: Mass Incarceration in the Age of Colorblindness*, is bringing a much-needed awareness to the prevalence and implications of racial disparities within the American criminal justice system. This has appropriately heightened concerns about ways that restorative justice may be contributing to or replicating these patterns. Has the field adequately monitored this possibility? Have we given enough thought to how restorative justice might be proactively used to address this problem? Have we adequately considered the possibility of built-in biases and assumptions in the way we articulate and practice restorative justice? Have we encouraged and listened to diverse voices about what restorative justice should involve? These are urgent questions that this book cannot answer; hopefully, though, it can be a catalyst for discussion.

Increasingly, the labels "victim" and "offender" are being questioned. While these terms provide handy shorthand references and are common within the criminal justice system, they also tend to oversimplify and stereotype. In criminology, labeling theory has emphasized that labels are often judgmental and people may tend to become what they are labeled. Also, in many situations such as in schools, responsibility for wrongdoing may be unclear, or some responsibility may be shared by all participants; "victim" and "offender" labels may be especially inappropriate in these contexts. The alternates to these simple labels are often awkward, but in this edition, I have tried to minimize the use of these terms though I have not eliminated them.

One area of controversy has been the terminology of the overall field: should it be restorative *justice* or restorative *practices*? Restorative approaches are being used in many situations such as in schools or for problem-solving where the terminology of "justice" may not seem appropriate. I am pleased to see these applications and readily acknowledge the limits of the "justice" language. However, in my experience, most conflicts and harms involve an experience or perception of injustice, and I prefer not to lose awareness of the justice dimension. Thus I continue to use the term restorative "justice" in this book while acknowledging that restorative "practices" may be appropriate in some contexts.

Now, on to what, in my view, restorative justice is *not*.

Restorative justice *is not...*

- ***Restorative justice is not primarily about forgiveness or reconciliation.***

Some victims and victim advocates react negatively to restorative justice because they imagine that the goal of such programs is to encourage, or even to coerce, them to forgive or reconcile with those who have caused them and/or their loved ones harm.

As we shall see, forgiveness or reconciliation is not a primary principle or focus of restorative justice. It is true that restorative justice does provide a context where either or both might happen. Indeed, some degree of forgiveness or even reconciliation—or at least a lessening of hostilities and fears—does seem to occur more frequently than in the adversarial setting of the criminal justice system. However, this is an experience that varies from participant to participant; it is entirely up to the individual. There should be no pressure to forgive or to seek reconciliation. Neither forgiveness nor reconciliation is a prerequisite to or a necessary outcome of restorative processes.

- *Restorative justice does not necessarily imply a return to past circumstances.*

  The term "restorative" is sometimes controversial because it can seem to imply a return to the past, as if the wrong or injury had not occurred. This is not likely to be possible, especially in the case of severe harm. Lynn Shiner, whose children were murdered, says "re-" words don't work: "I can't reorder anything because if I did, I would just pick up the scrambled pieces and put them back in order.... You build, you create a new life. I have a couple of pieces from my old life that I have to fit in."[1]

  In reality, a return to the past is rarely possible or even desirable. A person with a history of abuse or trauma or a long pattern of wrongdoing, for example, may not have a healthy personal or relational state to which to return. Their situation needs to be transformed, not restored. Similarly, restorative justice aims to transform, not perpetuate, patterns of racism and oppression.

  Restorative justice often involves movement toward a new sense of identity and health or new, healthier relationships. Many advocates see it as a way to restore a sense of hope and community to our world. In a recent email to me, restorative justice practitioner and attorney Fania Davis put it like this:

  > "It's not about returning to the pre-conflict status quo but about returning to one's best self that's always been there. When well facilitated, RJ processes create the possibility for transformation

of people, relationships, and communities. This is often a radical departure from the pre-conflict status quo. So what are we restoring? For me it's about returning to the part of us that really wants to be connected to one another in a good way. Returning to the goodness inherent in all of us. One might say returning to the divinity present in all of us. Or as indigenous elders put it, returning to that part of us which is related to all things."

- *Restorative justice is not mediation.*

Like mediation programs, many restorative justice programs are designed around the possibility of a facilitated meeting or encounter between those harmed and those who caused harm, as well as perhaps some family and community members. However, an encounter is not always chosen or appropriate. Moreover, restorative approaches are important even when an offending party has not been identified or apprehended or when a party is unwilling or unable to meet. So restorative approaches are not limited to an encounter.

Even when an encounter occurs, the term "mediation" is not a fitting description of that encounter. In a mediated conflict or dispute, parties are assumed to be on a level moral playing field, often with responsibilities that may need to be shared on all sides. While this sense of shared blame may be true in some criminal cases, in many cases it is not. Victims of rape or even burglaries do not want to be known as "disputants." In fact, they may well be struggling to overcome a tendency to blame themselves.

At any rate, to participate in most restorative justice encounters, a wrongdoer must admit to some level of responsibility for the offense, and an important component of such programs is to name and acknowledge the wrongdoing. The "neutral" language of mediation may be misleading and even offensive in many cases.

Although the term "mediation" was adopted early on in the restorative justice field, it is increasingly being replaced by terms such as "conferencing" or "dialogue" for the reasons outlined above.

- **Restorative justice is not primarily designed to reduce recidivism or repeat offenses.**

  In an effort to gain acceptance, restorative justice programs are often promoted or evaluated as ways to decrease repeat crimes.

  There are good reasons to believe that, in fact, such programs will reduce offending. Indeed, the research thus far is quite encouraging on this issue. Nevertheless, reduced recidivism is not the primary reason for operating restorative justice programs.

  Reduced recidivism is a byproduct, but restorative justice is done first of all because it is the right thing to do. Those who have suffered harm *should* be able to identify their needs and have them addressed; those who cause harm *should* be encouraged to take responsibility; and those affected by an offense *should* be involved in the process, regardless of whether the offending party gets the message and reduces their offending.

- **Restorative justice is not a particular program or a blueprint.**

  Various programs embody restorative justice in part or in full. However, there is no pure model that can be seen as ideal or that can be simply implemented in any community. Even after more than three decades of experience, we are still on a steep learning curve in this field. The most exciting practices that have emerged were not even imagined by those of us who began the first programs, and many more new ideas will surely emerge through dialogue and experimentation.

Also, all models are to some extent culture-bound. Consequently, restorative justice should be built from the bottom up, by communities, through dialogue, assessing their needs and resources, and applying the principles to their own situations.

> **Restorative justice is a compass, not a map.**

Restorative justice is *not a map*, but the principles of restorative justice can be seen as a *compass* offering direction. At a minimum, restorative justice is an invitation for dialogue and exploration.

- *Restorative justice is not limited to "minor" offenses or first-time offenders.*

  It may be easier to get community support for programs that address so-called "minor" cases. However, experience has shown that restorative approaches may have the greatest impact in more severe cases. Moreover, if the principles of restorative justice are taken seriously, the need for restorative approaches is especially clear in severe cases. The guiding questions of restorative justice (see page 51) may help to tailor justice responses in very difficult situations. Domestic violence is one of the most challenging areas of application, and great caution is advised. Yet successful restorative approaches are emerging in this area as well.

Restorative approaches are challenging in all offenses where there are significant power imbalances, including hate crimes, bullying, and child sexual abuse. Program design must take this into account, and facilitators need to be thoroughly cross-trained in the underlying issues that give rise to the violence. But it can be done, and many argue that, when done well, it can produce better results than the way the current system is trying to resolve these issues.

It may seem that restorative justice programs are most appropriate for young people. However, restorative justice is equally applicable to adults, and many programs are designed for both.

• *Restorative justice is not a new or North American development.*

The modern field of restorative justice developed in the 1970s from pilot projects in several North American communities. Seeking to apply their faith as well as their peace perspective to the harsh world of criminal justice, Mennonites and other practitioners (in Ontario, and later in Indiana) experimented with victim-offender encounters that led to programs in these communities and later became models for programs throughout the world. Restorative justice theory developed initially from these particular efforts.

However, the restorative justice movement did not develop out of a vacuum. It owes a great deal to earlier movements and to a variety of cultural and religious traditions. Many indigenous traditions had, and have, important restorative elements. The field owes a special debt to the Native people of North America and New Zealand for their contributions to the early development of the field, and other traditions are increasingly offering inspiration as well. The precedents and roots of restorative justice are much wider and deeper than the initiatives of the 1970s; they reach far back into human history.

- *Restorative justice is neither a panacea nor necessarily a replacement for the legal system.*

  Restorative justice, as it is currently practiced, is by no means an answer to all situations. Nor is it clear that it should replace the legal system, even in an ideal world. Many feel that even if restorative justice could be widely implemented, some form of the Western legal system (ideally, a restoratively-oriented one) would still be needed as a backup and guardian of basic

  > **Restorative justice highlights personal and interpersonal dimensions of crime.**

  human rights. Indeed, this is the function that the youth courts play in the restorative juvenile justice system of New Zealand.

  Most restorative justice advocates agree that crime has both a public dimension and a private dimension. Perhaps it would be more accurate to say that crime has a societal dimension, as well as a more personal and interpersonal dimension. The legal system focuses on the public dimension; that is, on society's interests and obligations as represented by the state. However, this emphasis downplays or ignores the personal and interpersonal aspects of crime. By putting a spotlight on and elevating the personal, interpersonal, and community dimensions of crime, restorative justice seeks to provide a better balance in how we experience justice.

- *Restorative justice is not necessarily an alternative to prison.*

  Western society, and especially the United States, greatly overuses prisons. If restorative justice were taken seriously, our reliance on prisons would be reduced, and the nature of prisons would change significantly. However, restorative justice approaches may sometimes be used in conjunction with, or parallel to, prison sentences. Restorative justice can be an alternative to prison and, as such, could reduce our over-reliance on prison. It does not necessarily eliminate the need for some form of incarceration in some cases, however.

- *Restorative justice is not necessarily the opposite of retribution.*

  Despite my earlier writing, I no longer see restoration as the polar opposite of retribution, though it should reduce our reliance on punishment for its own sake. More on that later on page 77.

Restorative justice *is* concerned about needs and roles

The restorative justice movement originally began as an effort to rethink the needs that crimes create as well as the roles implicit in crimes. Restorative justice advocates were concerned about needs that were not being met in the usual justice process. They also believed that the prevailing understanding of who the legitimate participants or stakeholders are in justice was too restrictive.

Restorative justice expands the circle of stakeholders—those with a stake or standing in the event or the case—beyond just the government and the offending party to include those who have been directly victimized as well as community members.

Because this view of needs and roles was at the origin of the movement, and because the needs/roles framework is so basic to the concept, it is important to start this review there. As the field has developed, stakeholder analysis has become more complex and encompassing.

> **Restorative justice expands the circle of stakeholders.**

The following discussion is limited to some of the core concerns that were present at the beginning of the movement and that continue to play a central role. It is also limited to "justice needs"—the needs of those harmed, of those causing harm, and of community members—that might be met, at least partially, through a justice process.

Victims: those who have been harmed

Of special concern to restorative justice in a criminal justice context are the needs of crime victims that are not being adequately met by the criminal justice system. People who have been victimized often feel ignored, neglected, or even abused by the justice process. Sometimes, in fact, the state's interests are in direct conflict with those of victims. This results in part from the legal definition of crime, which does not directly include victims themselves. Crime is defined as against the state, so the state takes the place of the victims. Yet those who have been harmed often have a number of specific needs from the justice process.

Due to the legal definition of crime and the nature of the criminal justice process, the following four types of needs seem to be especially neglected:

1. **Information**. Those who have experienced harm need answers to questions they have about the offense or the offender, including why and how the offense happened and what has happened since. They need *real* information, not speculation or the legally constrained information that comes from a trial or plea agreement. Securing real information usually requires direct or indirect access to the one who caused the harm and holds this information.

2. **Truth-telling**. An important element in healing or transcending the experience of crime is an opportunity to tell the story of what happened. There are good therapeutic reasons for this. Part of the trauma of crime is the way it upsets our views of ourselves and our world—our life-stories. Transcendence of these experiences means "re-storying" our lives by telling the stories in significant settings, often where they can receive public acknowledgment. Often, too, it is important for those victimized to tell their stories to the ones who caused the harm and to have them understand the impact of their actions.

3. **Empowerment**. People who have been victimized often feel like control has been taken

away from them by the offenses they've experienced—control over their properties, their bodies, their emotions, their dreams. Involvement in their own cases as they go through the justice process can be an important way to return a sense of empowerment to them. The opportunity and encouragement to self-identify their own needs is also important—rather than have them defined by the state or even victim advocates.

4. **Restitution or vindication**. Restitution by those who have caused harm is often important to those harmed, sometimes because of the actual losses, but just as importantly, because of the symbolic recognition restitution implies. When someone who has caused harm makes an effort to make right the harm, even if only partially, it is a way of saying, "I am taking responsibility, and you are not to blame."

Restitution, in fact, is a symptom or sign of a more basic need, the need for vindication. While the concept of vindication is beyond the

> Victims should be able to identify their own needs.

scope of this booklet, I am convinced that it is a basic need that we all have when we are treated unjustly. Restitution is one of a number of ways of meeting this need to even the score. Apology may also help meet this need to have one's harm recognized.

The theory and practice of restorative justice have emerged from and been profoundly shaped by an effort to take these "justice needs" of victims seriously.[2]

Offenders: those who have caused harm

A second major area of concern that gave rise to restorative justice is ensuring accountability for those who have caused harm.

The criminal justice system is concerned about holding offenders accountable, but accountability in that system means making sure those who cause harm get the punishment they deserve. Little in the process encourages them to understand the consequences of their actions or to empathize with those they have harmed. On the contrary, the adversarial game requires them to look out for themselves. Those who have offended are discouraged from acknowledging their responsibility and are given little opportunity to act on this responsibility in concrete ways. Indeed, the risk of lengthy prison sentences acts as a disincentive to truth telling.

The neutralizing strategies—the stereotypes and rationalizations that those who offend often use to distance themselves from the people they hurt—are never challenged. Unfortunately, then, their sense of alienation from society is only heightened by the legal process and by the prison experience; indeed, they often feel like victims of the system and society. For a variety of reasons, then, the legal process tends to discourage responsibility and empathy on the part of those who have offended.

Restorative justice has brought an awareness of the limits and negative byproducts of punishment. Beyond that, however, it has argued that punishment is not real accountability. Real accountability involves facing up to what one has done. It means encouraging those who have caused harm to understand the impact of their behavior—the harms they have done—and urging them to take steps to put things as right as possible. This accountability, it is argued, is better for those who have been victimized, better for those who have caused harm, and better for society as well.

Those who have caused harm have other needs beyond their responsibilities to victims and communities. If we expect them to assume their responsibilities, to change their behavior, and to become contributing members of our communities, their needs, says restorative justice, must be addressed as well. That subject is beyond the scope of this *Little Book*, but the following suggests some of what is needed.

Those who have caused harm need justice to provide:

1. Accountability
    *   that addresses the resulting harms,
    *   encourages empathy and responsibility,
    *   and transforms shame.[3]

2. Encouragement to experience personal transformation including
    *   healing for the harms that contributed to their offending behavior, including personal and historical traumas;[4]
    *   opportunities for treatment for addictions and/or other problems;
    *   and enhancement of personal competencies.

3. Encouragement and support for integration into the community.

4. For a small number, at least temporary restraint.

Community

Communities and their members have needs arising from crime, and they have roles to play. Restorative justice advocates, such as former judge Barry Stuart and Kay Pranis, argue that when the state takes over in our name, it undermines our sense of community.[5] Communities are impacted by crime and, in many cases, should be considered stakeholders as secondary victims. Communities may also have responsibilities to victims, to offenders, and to others who are part of the community.

When a community becomes involved in a case, it can initiate a forum to work at these matters, while strengthening the community itself. This topic, too, is a large one. The following list suggests some areas of concern.

Communities need justice to provide:

1. Attention to their concerns as victims.

2. Opportunities to build a sense of community and mutual accountability.

3. Opportunities and encouragement to take on their obligations for the welfare of their members, including those who have been harmed and those who caused harm, and to foster the conditions that promote healthy communities.

Much more has been written about who has a **stake** in a crime and about their needs and roles. However, the **basic** concerns about the needs and roles of victims, **offe**nders, and community members outlined above **con-tinue** to provide the focus for both the theory and practice of restorative justice.

> **Restorative justice focuses on needs more than deserts.**

In short, the legal or criminal justice system centers on offenders and deserts—making sure those who offend get what they *deserve*. Restorative justice is more focused on *needs*: the needs of those harmed, of those causing harm, and of the communities in which these situations arise.

CHAPTER 2

Restorative Principles

Restorative justice is based upon an old, common-sense understanding of wrongdoing. Although it would be expressed differently in different cultures, this approach is probably common to most traditional societies. For those of us from a European background, it is the way many of our ancestors (and perhaps even our parents) understood wrongdoing.

- *"Crime" or wrongdoing is a violation of people and of interpersonal relationships.*

- *Violations create obligations.*

- *The central obligation is to put right the wrongs, i.e., to repair the harms caused by wrongdoing.*

Underlying this understanding of wrongdoing is an assumption about society: we are all interconnected. In the Hebrew scriptures, this is embedded in the concept of *shalom*, the vision of living in a sense of "all-rightness" with each other, with the creator, and with the environment. Many cultures have a word that represents this notion of the centrality of relationships. For the Maori, it is communicated by *whakapapa*; for the Navajo, *hozho*; for many Africans, the Bantu word *ubuntu*; for Tibetan Buddhists, *tendrel*. Although the specific meanings of these words vary, they communicate a similar message: all things are connected to each other in a web of relationships.

In this worldview, the problem of crime—and wrongdoing in general—is that it represents a wound in the community, a tear in the web of relationships. Crime represents damaged relationships. In fact, damaged relationships are both a *cause* and an *effect* of crime. Many traditions have a saying that a harm

> A harm to one is a harm to all.

to one is a harm to all. A harm such as crime ripples out to disrupt the whole web. Moreover, wrongdoing is often a symptom of something that is out of balance in the web.

Interrelationships imply mutual obligations and responsibilities. It comes as no surprise, then, that this view of wrongdoing emphasizes the importance of making amends or of "putting right." Indeed, making amends for wrongdoing is an obligation. While the initial emphasis may be on the obligations owed by those who have caused harm, the focus on interconnectedness opens the possibility that others—especially the larger community—may have obligations as well.

Even more fundamentally, this view of wrongdoing implies a concern for healing of those involved—those directly harmed, those who cause harm, and their communities.

How does this understanding compare or contrast with the "legal" or criminal justice understanding of crime? The differences in these two approaches might be boiled down to three central questions asked in the search for justice as shown in the accompanying chart.

Two different views

Criminal justice	Restorative justice
• Crime is a violation of the law and the state.	• Crime is a violation of people and relationships.
• Violations create guilt.	• Violations create obligations.
• Justice requires the state to determine blame (guilt) and impose pain (punishment).	• Justice involves victims, offenders, and community members in an effort to repair the harm, to "put things right."
• *Central focus: offenders getting what they deserve.*	• *Central focus: victim needs and offender responsibility for repairing harm.*

Three different questions

Criminal justice	Restorative justice
• What laws have been broken? • Who did it? • What do they deserve?	• Who has been harmed? • What are their needs? • Whose obligations are these?

In an oft-quoted passage from Christian and Jewish scripture, the prophet Micah asks the question, "What does the Lord require?" The answer begins with the phrase, "To do justice." But what does justice require? As we have seen, Western society's answer has focused on making sure those who have offended get what they deserve. *Restorative justice answers differently, focusing first of all on needs and associated obligations.*

Appendix I provides a fuller statement of restorative justice principles and their implications, based directly on the concept of wrongdoing outlined above. For our purposes here, however, the concept of interrelatedness is basic to understanding why needs, roles, and obligations are so essential to restorative justice.

Three pillars of restorative justice

Three central concepts or pillars deserve a closer look: *harms and needs, obligations,* and *engagement.*

1. Restorative justice focuses on *harm.*

Restorative justice understands crime first of all as harm done to people and communities. Our legal system, with its focus on rules and laws and with its view that the state is the victim, often loses sight of this reality.

Concerned primarily with making sure those who offend get what they deserve, the legal system usually considers those victimized as, at best, a secondary concern of justice. Focusing on harm, on the contrary, implies an inherent concern for the needs and roles of those who have been harmed.

For restorative justice, then, justice begins with a concern for victims and their needs. It seeks to repair the harm as much as possible, both concretely and symbolically. This victim-oriented approach requires that justice be concerned about victims' needs even when no offender has been identified or apprehended. And it is important that those who have been harmed are provided an opportunity to define

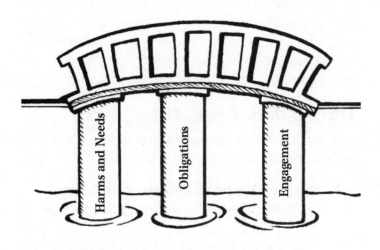

their needs rather than having others or a system define needs for them.

While our first concern must be the harm experienced by victims, the focus on harm implies that we also need to be concerned about harms experienced by those who have caused the harm as well as communities. This may require us to address the root causes of crime. The goal of restorative justice is to provide an experience of healing for all concerned. And ideally, restorative justice is about prevention of harm as well as justice after harm has occurred.

2. Wrongs or harms result in *obligations*.

For this reason, restorative justice emphasizes accountability and responsibility for those who cause harm.

The legal system defines accountability as making sure those who offend are punished. If crime is essentially about harm, however, accountability means they should be encouraged to understand that harm. Those who have caused harm should begin to comprehend the consequences of their behavior. Moreover, it means they have a responsibility to repair the harm, making things right as much as possible, both concretely and symbolically. That is, they have a responsibility to do right by the people they harmed. This is not only the "right" thing to do but is more likely than punishment to deter future offending.

As we shall see, the first obligation is on those who are directly responsible for the harm, but the community and society have obligations as well.

3. Restorative justice promotes *engagement or participation.*

The principle of engagement suggests that the primary parties affected by crime—those who have been victimized, those who have offended, and members of the community—are provided significant roles in the justice process. These "stakeholders" need to be given information about each other and need to be involved in deciding what justice requires in this case.

In some cases, this may mean actual dialogue between these parties, as happens in victim offender conferences. They share their stories and come to a consensus about what should be done. In other cases, it may involve indirect exchanges, the use of surrogates, or other forms of involvement.

The principle of engagement implies involvement of an enlarged circle of parties as compared to the traditional justice process.

So restorative justice is constructed upon three simple elements or pillars: *harms and related needs* (of those victimized, first of all, but also of the communities and those who cause harm); *obligations* that have resulted from (and given rise to) this harm (offender's, but also the community's); and *engagement* of those who have a legitimate interest or stake in the offense and its resolution (those harmed, those causing harm, and community members). Ross London has argued that "the soul of RJ is the effort to repair the harm of crime."[1]

Below, in summary, is a skeletal outline of restorative justice. Although it is inadequate by itself, it provides a framework upon which a fuller understanding can be built.

> Restorative justice requires, at minimum, that we address the harms and needs of those harmed, hold those causing harm accountable to "put right" those harms, and involve both of these parties as well as relevant communities in this process.

The "how" and the "who" are important

Who is involved in the justice process, and how they are involved, is an important part of restorative justice.

Process—the "how"

Our legal system is an adversarial process conducted by professionals who stand in for the offender and the state, refereed by a judge. Outcomes are imposed by authorities—laws, judges, or juries—who stand outside the essential conflict. Victims, community members, and even offenders rarely participate in this process in any substantial way.

Although restorative justice usually recognizes the need for outside authorities and, in some cases, imposed outcomes, it prefers *processes that are collaborative and inclusive* and *outcomes that are mutually agreed upon rather than imposed.*

Restorative justice often acknowledges a place for the adversarial approach and the role of professionals as well as an important role for the state. However, restorative justice emphasizes the importance of participation by those who have a direct stake in the event or offense—that

> **Restorative justice prefers inclusive, collaborative processes and consensual outcomes.**

is, those who are involved, impacted by, or who otherwise have a legitimate interest in the offense.

A direct, facilitated, face-to-face encounter—with adequate screening, preparation, and safeguards—is often an ideal forum for the participation of the particular stakeholders. As we shall see shortly, this can take a variety of forms: a victim offender conference, a family group conference, or a circle process.

A meeting allows those harmed and those causing harm to give faces to each other, to ask questions of each other directly, to negotiate together how to put things right. It provides an opportunity for those who have been victimized to ask questions or to directly tell the one who victimized them the impact of the offense. It allows those who have offended to hear and to begin to understand the effects of their behavior. It offers possibilities for acceptance of responsibility and apology. Many of those who been victimized, as well as those who have offended, have found such a meeting to be a powerful and positive experience.

An encounter—direct or indirect—is not always possible, and, in some cases, may not be desirable. In some cultures, a direct encounter may be inappropriate. An indirect encounter might include a letter, a video exchange, or meeting with a person who represents the victim. In all cases, efforts should be made to provide maximum involvement of the stakeholders and exchange of information between them.

Stakeholders—the "who"

The key stakeholders, of course, are those who have been directly harmed and those who caused the harm. Members of the community may be directly affected, too, and thus should also be considered immediate stakeholders. In addition to this circle, there are others who have varying degrees of stake in the situation. These may include family members and friends of the victim or other "secondary victims"; families or friends of those who caused the harm; or other members of the community.

Who is the community?

Controversy has arisen within the restorative justice field about the meaning of community and how actually to involve the community in these processes. The issue is particularly a problem in cultures where traditional communities have eroded, as is true in much of the United States. Furthermore, "community" can be too abstract a concept to be useful. And a community can be guilty of abuses. A discussion of these issues is beyond the scope of this book, but a few observations may be helpful.[2]

In practice, restorative justice has tended to focus on "communities of care" or micro-communities. There are communities of *place*, where people live near and interact with each other, but there are also networks of relationships that are not geographically defined. For restorative justice, the key questions are: 1) who in the community cares about these people or about this offense, and 2) how can we involve them in the process?

It may be helpful to differentiate between "community" and "society." Restorative justice has tended to focus on the micro-communities of place or relationships that are directly affected by an offense but are often neglected by "state justice." However, there are larger concerns and obligations that belong to society beyond those who have a direct stake in a particular event. These include a society's concern for the safety, human rights, and general well-being of its members. Many argue that the government has an important and legitimate role in looking after such societal concerns.[3]

Restorative justice aims to put things right

We have discussed so far the needs and roles of stakeholders. More needs to be said, however, about the *goals* of restorative justice.

Addressing harm

Central to restorative justice is the idea of making things right or, to use a more active phrase often used in British English, "putting right." It is the opportunity and encouragement for those who have caused harm to do right by those they have harmed. As already noted, this implies a responsibility on the part of the offending person or persons to, as much as possible, take active steps to repair the harm to those harmed (and perhaps the impacted community). In cases such as murder, the harm obviously cannot be repaired; however, symbolic steps, including acknowledgment of responsibility or restitution, can be helpful to surviving family members and loved ones—or "co-victims"—and are a responsibility of offenders.

Putting right implies reparation or restoration or recovery, but these "re-" words are often inadequate. When a severe wrong has been committed, there is no possibility of repairing the harm or going back to what was before.

> **Restorative justice seeks to "make things right."**

It is possible that someone who has been harmed may be helped toward healing when the one causing the harm works toward making things right—whether concretely or symbolically. Many crime victims, however, are ambivalent about the term "healing," because of the sense of finality or termination that it connotes. This journey belongs to victims—no one else can walk it for them—but an effort to put right can assist in this process, although it can never fully restore.

The obligation to put right is first of all the responsibility of those who have caused the harm. However, the community may have responsibilities as well—to those harmed, but perhaps also to those causing harm. For those responsible for the harm to successfully carry out their obligations, they may need support and encouragement from the wider community. Moreover, the community has responsibilities for the situations that are causing or encouraging crime. Ideally, restorative justice processes can provide a catalyst and/or a forum for exploring and assigning these needs, responsibilities, and expectations.

Addressing causes

Putting right requires that we address the harms but also the *causes* of crime. Many people who have been victimized want this. They want to know that steps are being taken to reduce such harms to themselves and others.

Family group conferences in New Zealand, where restorative justice is the norm for youth justice, are expected to develop a consensually-supported plan that includes elements for both reparation and prevention. These plans must speak to the needs of those victimized and to the obligations of the offending person or persons to address those needs. But the plan must also address what those who have offended need in order to change their behaviors.

Those who offend have an obligation to address the causes of their behavior, but they usually cannot do this alone. Moreover, there may be larger obligations beyond those that are the direct responsibility of the one who has caused the harm. Social injustices and other conditions that cause crime or create unsafe conditions are in part the responsibility of families, communities, and the larger society.

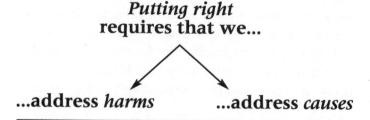

Putting right
requires that we...

...address *harms*   **...address *causes***

Offenders as victims

If we are to truly address harms and causes, we must explore the harms that those who cause harm have themselves experienced.

Studies show that many of those who offend have indeed been victimized or traumatized in significant ways. And even when they have not been directly victimized, many people who offend perceive themselves to be victims. These harms and perceptions of harms may be an important contributing cause of crime. In fact, Harvard professor and former prison psychiatrist James Gilligan has argued that all violence is an effort to achieve justice or to undo injustice.[4] In other words, much crime may be a response to—or an effort to undo—a sense of victimization.

A perception of oneself as victim does not absolve responsibility for offending behavior. However, if Gilligan is right, we cannot expect offending behavior to stop without addressing this sense of victimization. In fact, punishment often reinforces the sense of victimization.

Sometimes offenders are satisfied when their sense of being victims is simply acknowledged. Sometimes their perception of being victims must be challenged. Sometimes the damage done must be repaired before they can be expected to change their behavior.

This is a controversial topic and especially difficult, understandably, for those who have been victims of crime but have done little or no harm to others in their lives. Too often these reasoned arguments sound like excuses. Moreover, why do some people who are victimized turn to crime and others do not? Nevertheless, I am convinced that any attempt to reduce the causes of offending will require us to explore offenders' experiences of victimization.

In this exploration, instead of using the loaded language of victimization, it may be more helpful to speak of "trauma." In her book *Creating Sanctuary*, psychiatrist Sandra Bloom makes the point that unresolved trauma tends to be reenacted. If it is not adequately dealt with, trauma is reenacted in the lives of those who experience the trauma, in their families, even in future generations.[5]

Restorative justice balances concern for all.

Trauma is a core experience not only of those victimized, but also of many who offend. Much violence may actually be a reenactment of trauma that was experienced earlier but not responded to adequately. Society tends to respond by delivering more trauma in the form of imprisonment. While the realities of trauma must not be used to excuse, they must be understood, and they must be addressed.

In summary, an effort to put right the wrongs is the hub or core of restorative justice. Putting right has two dimensions: 1) addressing the harms that have been done, and 2) addressing the causes of those harms, including the contributing harms.

Since justice should seek to put right, and since victims have been harmed, *restorative justice must start with those who have been victimized* and their needs.

However, restorative justice is ultimately concerned about the restoration and reintegration of those who have been harmed, those who have caused harm, and the well-being of the entire community. Restorative justice is about balancing concern for all parties.

> Restorative justice encourages outcomes that promote responsibility, reparation, and healing for all.

A restorative lens

Restorative justice seeks to provide an alternate framework or lens for thinking about crime and justice.

Principles

This restorative lens or philosophy can be envisioned around five key principles or actions:

1. Focus on the harms and consequent needs of those harmed first of all, but also on those of the community and of those causing harm;

2. Address the obligations that result from those harms (the obligations of the offending persons, as well as those of the community and society);

3. Use inclusive, collaborative processes;

4. Involve those with a legitimate stake in the situation, including those victimized, those offending, community members, and society;

5. Seek to repair the harm and put right the wrongs to the extent possible.

We might diagram restorative justice as a wheel. At the hub is the central focus of restorative justice: seeking to put right the wrongs and harms. Each of the spokes represents the four other essential elements outlined above: focusing on harms and needs, addressing obligations, involving stakeholders (victims, offenders, and communities), and, to the extent possible, using collaborative, inclusive processes. This needs to be done, of course, in an attitude of respect for all involved.

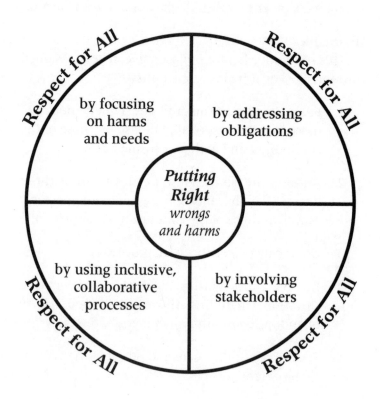

To use an image that is more organic, we might diagram restorative justice as a flower. In the center is the central focus: putting right. Each of the petals represents one of the principles required to succeed in putting right.

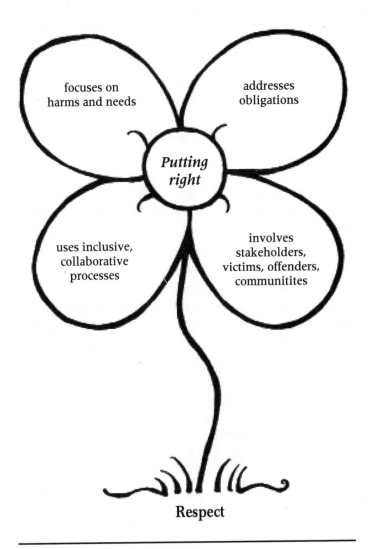

Respect

Values

The principles of restorative justice are useful only if they are rooted in a number of underlying values. Too often these values are unstated and taken for granted. However, to apply restorative justice principles in a way that is true to their spirit and intent, we must be explicit about these values. Otherwise, for example, we might use a restoratively-based process but arrive at non-restorative outcomes.

The principles of restorative justice—the hub and the spokes—must be surrounded by a rim of values in order to function properly. The principles that make up the restorative justice flower must be rooted in values in order to flourish.

As I noted earlier, underlying restorative justice is the vision of interconnectedness. Whether we realize it or not, we are all connected to each other and to the larger world through a web of relationships. When this web is disrupted, we are all affected. The primary elements of restorative justice—harm and need, obligation, and participation—derive from this vision.

But as Jarem Sawatsky has pointed out, this value of interconnectedness must be balanced by an appreciation for particularity.[6] Although we are connected, we are not the same. Particularity appreciates diversity. It respects the individuality and worth of each person. It takes seriously specific contexts and situations.

Justice must acknowledge both our interconnections and our individuality. The value of particularity reminds us that context, culture, and personality are all important.

Much more could be and has been written about the values underlying restorative justice. In fact, perhaps one of restorative justice's greatest attributes is the way it encourages us to explore our values together.

Ultimately, however, one basic value is supremely important: respect. If I had to put restorative justice into one word, I would choose respect: respect for all—even those who are different from us, even those who seem to be our enemies. Respect reminds us of our interconnectedness but also of our differences. Respect insists that we balance concern for all parties. Respect can help us to recognize and address unjust hierarchies of power.

> **Restorative justice is respect.**

If we pursue justice as respect, treating all equally, we will do justice restoratively.

If we do not respect others, we will not do justice restoratively, no matter how earnestly we adopt the principles.

The value of respect underlies restorative justice principles and must guide and shape their application.

Defining restorative justice

How, then, should restorative justice be defined? Even though there is general agreement on the basic outlines of restorative justice, those in the field have been unable to come to a consensus on its specific meaning. Some of us question the wisdom or usefulness of such a definition. While we recognize the need for principles and benchmarks, we worry about the arrogance and finality of establishing a rigid meaning. With these concerns in mind, I offer the following as a working definition of restorative justice.[7]

> Restorative justice is an approach to achieving justice that involves, to the extent possible, those who have a stake in a specific offense or harm to collectively identify and address harms, needs, and obligations in order to heal and put things as right as possible.

The goals of restorative justice

In her excellent handbook, *Restorative Justice: A Vision for Healing and Change,* Susan Sharpe summarizes the goals and tasks of restorative justice in this way:[8]

Restorative justice programs aim to:

- *put key decisions into the hands of those most affected by crime;*

- *make justice more healing and, ideally, more transformative;*

- *reduce the likelihood of future offenses.*

Achieving these goals requires that:

- *victims are involved in the process and come out of it satisfied;*

- *offenders understand how their actions have affected other people and take responsibility for those actions;*

- *outcomes help to repair the harms done and address the reasons for the offenses (specific plans are tailored to the victims' and the offenders' needs);*

- *victims and offenders both gain a sense of "closure,"* [9] *and both are reintegrated into the community.*

Guiding questions of restorative justice

Ultimately, restorative justice boils down to a set of questions that we need to ask when a wrong occurs. These guiding questions are, in fact, the essence of restorative justice.

Guiding questions of restorative justice

1. Who has been harmed?

2. What are their needs?

3. Whose obligations are these?

4. Who has a stake in this situation?

5. What are the causes?

6. What is the appropriate process to involve stakeholders in an effort to put things right and address underlying causes?

If we think of restorative justice as a particular program, or a set of programs, we soon find it difficult to apply those programs to a broad variety of situations. For example, the forms of victim offender conferencing being used for "ordinary" crimes may have little direct application in cases of mass, societal violence. Without careful safeguards, restorative justice models of practice may be dangerous if applied to situations of patterned violence and imbalances of power like domestic violence.

If we instead employ the guiding questions that shape restorative justice, we find restorative justice to be applicable to a wide range of situations. The guiding questions of restorative justice can help us to reframe issues, to think beyond the confines that legal justice has created for society, and to "change our lenses" on wrongdoing.

These guiding questions are causing some defense attorneys in the U.S. to rethink their roles and obligations in death penalty cases. Defense victim outreach (DVO, formerly DIVO) has emerged as an effort to incorporate survivors' needs and concerns in trials and their outcomes by giving survivors access to the defense, as well as the prosecution. This approach also seeks to encourage defendants to take appropriate responsibility in these cases. A number of plea agreements have been reached that were based on victims' needs and that allowed offenders to accept responsibility.

Many victim advocates are deeply concerned about the dangers of victim-offender encounters in situations of domestic violence. These concerns are legitimate; there are profound dangers in an encounter where a pattern of violence continues or where cases are not being carefully monitored by people trained in domestic violence. Some would argue that encounters are never appropriate. Others, including some victims of domestic violence, argue that encounters are important and powerful in the right situations and with appropriate safeguards. In recent years, successful programs using a restorative approach have been developed in some communities.

But whether or not encounters are appropriate in situations like domestic violence, the guiding questions of restorative justice can help sort out what needs to be done without getting stuck on—and limited to—the question, "What does the offender deserve?" When faced with a new situation or

> **Restorative justice involves changing our questions.**

application, I often turn to these questions as a guide.

The guiding questions of restorative justice may, in fact, be viewed as restorative justice in a nutshell.

Signposts of restorative justice

As we begin to think of practical applications of restorative justice, another guide is provided by the following ten principles or signposts. These principles can be of use in designing or evaluating programs. Like the guiding questions, they may be useful in crafting responses to specific cases or situations.

Signposts of restorative justice[10]

1. Focus on the harms of wrongdoing rather than the rules that have been broken.

2. Show equal concern and commitment to those victimized and those who have offended, involving both in the process of justice.

3. Work toward the restoration of those harmed, empowering them and responding to their needs as they see them.

4. Support those who have offended, while encouraging them to understand, accept, and carry out their obligations.

5. Recognize that while obligations may be difficult for those who have offended, those obligations should not be intended as harms, and they must be achievable.

6. Provide opportunities for dialogue, direct or indirect, between those harmed and those who have harmed, as desired by both parties.

7. Find meaningful ways to involve the community and to respond to the community bases of crime.

8. Encourage collaboration and reintegration of both those who are harmed and those who harmed, rather than relying upon coercion and isolation.

9. Give attention to the unintended consequences of actions and programs.

10. Show respect to all parties—those harmed, those who harmed, their friends and loved ones, and justice colleagues.

CHAPTER 3

Restorative
Practices

T he concept and philosophy of restorative justice
emerged during the 1970s and '80s in the United
States and Canada in conjunction with a practice
that was then called the Victim Offender Reconciliation
Program (VORP). Since then, VORP has been modi-
fied and usually renamed, new forms of practice have
appeared, and older programs have been reshaped and
renamed "restorative." What are the main approaches or
practices currently being used within the Western criminal justice field? Be aware that the applications in the
criminal justice arena that I cite here are by no means
the whole picture.

Schools have become an important area of restorative practices. While there are some similarities to restorative justice programs for criminal cases, the approaches used in an educational setting must necessarily be shaped to fit that context. (Two *Little Books* in this series address these settings; see Additional Reading at the end of this book.)

Restorative approaches are also being adapted to the workplace and to larger community issues and processes. Again, there are similarities to the models outlined below, but there are also important differences. Restorative justice also has become part of the conversation about how to approach "transitional justice," e.g., following large-scale, societal conflicts and wrongdoing. The focus below, however, is on approaches in a criminal justice context.

For those who come from societies closer to traditional ways—in Africa, for example, or in North American indigenous communities—restorative justice often serves as a catalyst to reevaluate, resurrect, legitimate, and adapt older, customary approaches. During colonization, the Western legal model often condemned and repressed traditional forms of justice that, although not perfect, were highly functional for those societies.

Restorative justice can provide a conceptual framework to affirm and legitimate what was good about those traditions and to develop adapted models that can operate within the realities of the modern legal system. In fact, two of the most important forms of restorative justice—family group conferences and peacemaking circles—are adaptations (but not replications) of these traditional ways.

Restorative justice is also providing a concrete way to think about justice within the theory and practice of conflict transformation and peacebuilding. Most conflicts revolve around, or at least involve, a sense of injustice. Although the field of conflict resolution or conflict transformation has acknowledged

> **Restorative justice aids conflict transformation and peacebuilding.**

this somewhat, the concept and practice of justice in this area has been fairly vague. The principles and practices of restorative justice can provide a concrete framework for addressing justice issues within a conflict. (See Appendix V.)

For example, after taking a restorative justice course in our Summer Peacebuilding Institute, several African practitioners returned to Ghana where they had previously been trying to help resolve a protracted conflict. Drawing upon the restorative justice framework, they were able, for the first time, to address the justice issues in the conflict, using their traditional community justice process. As a result, the peacemaking effort came unstuck and began to move forward.

Similarly, several Pakistani practitioners who graduated from our program have returned to Pakistan and found the restorative justice model helpful for enlightening and updating their traditional *jirga* process for decision-making and conflict resolution.

The restorative justice field is becoming too diverse to capture it in any simple classification. Moreover, the various models described below are often blended, making clear distinctions between them difficult. The following, however, is an attempt to provide a brief overview of some of its emerging practices within the Western criminal justice arena. A separate *Little Book* is available for each of these models, describing them in much more detail. (See Additional Reading.)

Core approaches often involve a facilitated encounter

Three distinct models have tended to dominate the practice of restorative justice: victim offender conferences, family group conferences, and circle processes. Increasingly, however, these models are being blended. Family group conferences may utilize a circle, and new forms with elements of each are being developed for certain circumstances. In some cases, several models may be used in a single case or situation. A victim offender encounter may be held prior to and in preparation for a sentencing circle, for example.

All of these models have important elements in common, however. Each of these models involves a

Models are often blended.

facilitated encounter or dialogue between key stakeholders—those harmed and those causing harm, at minimum, and perhaps other community and justice people as well. Sometimes, if an encounter between a victim and an offender is impossible or inappropriate, representatives or surrogates may be used. Sometimes letters or videos are used in preparation for, or in place of, a direct meeting. All of these models, however, involve some form of encounter and dialogue, with a preference for face-to-face meetings.

These encounters are led by trained facilitators who guide the process, balancing concern for all the parties involved. Unlike arbitrators, conference or circle facilitators do not impose settlements. Each model allows an opportunity for participants to explore facts, feelings, and resolutions. They are encouraged to tell their stories, to ask questions, to express their feelings, and to work toward mutually acceptable outcomes.

Ron Claassen, a longtime restorative justice practitioner, has noted that to resolve any type of wrongdoing, three things have to happen:[1]

1. The wrong or injustice must be acknowledged;

2. Equity needs to be created or restored;

3. Future intentions need to be addressed.

An encounter provides an opportunity for the wrongdoing to be articulated by those harmed and acknowledged by those who caused the harm. Outcomes such as restitution or apology help to right the balance— that is, to establish or restore equity.

Questions about the future usually need to be discussed: Will the person who caused harm do this again? How do we live together in the same community? How do we move ahead with life? All restorative conferencing models provide for such questions to be addressed through the facilitated encounter.

> **Victim participation must be fully voluntary.**

In each of these models, participation by the one who has been harmed must be entirely voluntary. In each, a prerequisite is that the person who caused the harm acknowledges, at least to some extent, his or her responsibility. Normally, conferences are not held if the offending person denies all responsibility, though often they do not acknowledge full responsibility prior to the conference.

Efforts are made to maximize the offending person's voluntary participation as well. Certainly conferences should not be held if he or she is unwilling and uncooperative. In reality, however, there is often some pressure on the offending person to choose between lesser evils. In interviews, those who have offended often suggest that it is difficult and frightening to face the ones they have harmed. Indeed, most of us would try to avoid such obligations if we could.

With the exception of the New Zealand family group conferences, the models described below are usually used on a discretionary, referral basis. For lesser offenses, referrals sometimes come from the community, perhaps from a school or religious institution. Occasionally, referrals are generated by the parties themselves.

Most referrals, however, come from within the justice system with the exact referral point varying with the case and the community. Cases may be referred by the police, by the prosecutor, by probation, by the court, even by prisons. In the case of a court referral, it may be after adjudication but before sentencing. In such instances, the judge takes the outcome of the conference into account in the sentence. In some cases or jurisdictions, the judge orders restitution and asks that the amount be established through a restorative conference. The agreement then becomes part of the sentence and/or the probation order.

A number of communities are now encouraging some form of restorative encounter to happen much earlier in the process, before charges have been formally brought, as a way of keeping cases out of the system. In Concord, Massachusetts, Communities for Restorative Justice represents a partnership between the police and the community and is making this possible for a variety of cases.

Originally established to help address racial disparities in the juvenile justice system in Oakland, California, pre-charge conferences based on New Zealand's model are diverting rather serious offenses out of the system by providing accountability as well as support from families and the community. With the agreement of the prosecutor, this program is able to make a "reverse Miranda" statement to the offending person, i.e., that nothing said in the conference will be used against him or her.

In one high-profile murder case in Florida, a pre-charge conference allowed the family members of the young woman who was killed, the young man who was responsible along with his family, the prosecutor, and the defense attorney to meet together to address the issues noted above and to work toward a consensus on the sentence that would be part of a plea agreement.[2]

In the U.S., however, most current programs for victim-offender encounters in cases of severe violence are outside the formal justice system and are designed to be initiated by the parties themselves, most commonly by those who have been victimized or their loved ones. At least half of U.S. states now have protocols and/or programs in place for victims who wish to participate.

Models differ in the "who" and the "how"

Although similar in basic outline, the models of restorative justice practice differ in the number and category of participants and, in some cases, the style of facilitation.

Victim offender conferences

Victim offender conferences (VOC) involve primarily those directly harmed and those responsible for the harm. Upon referral, the two parties are first worked with individually. Then, upon their agreement to proceed, they are brought together in a meeting or conference. The meeting is put together and led by a trained facilitator or co-facilitators who guide the process in a balanced manner.

A signed restitution agreement is often an outcome, although this is less likely to be true in cases of severe violence. Family members of either party may participate, but they are usually seen as having secondary, supporting roles. Persons representing the community may be involved as facilitators and/or program overseers, but they do not usually participate in meetings.

Family group conferences

Family group conferences (FGC) enlarge the circle of primary participants to include family members or other individuals significant to the parties directly involved. Because this model has tended to focus on supporting those who have offended in taking responsibility and changing their behavior, the offending person's family and/or other relevant people from the community are especially important. However, family and supporters of those harmed are invited as well. In some circumstances, and especially when the FGC is empowered to affect the legal outcome of the case, a justice person such as a police officer may be present.

Two basic forms of family group conferences have gained prominence. One model that has received considerable attention in North America was initially developed by police in Australia, based in part on ideas from New Zealand. Often this approach has used a standardized, "scripted" model of facilitation. Facilitators may be authority figures such as specially trained police officers, although though this has been controversial, especially in communities where relationships with police are strained.

This tradition or approach has given special attention to the dynamics of shame and often actively attempts to use shame in a positive way. The proactive use of shame is a highly controversial subject, however. Some argue that shame is too volatile and dangerous to encourage address-ing it in a conference, even though it is very likely to be present, often for both parties.

> **Successful conferences involve managing rather than promoting shame.**

The success of conferences seems to hinge on the suc-cessful management and transformation of shame rather than the deliberate encouragement of shame.

The older model of FGCs, and the one with which I am more familiar, originated in New Zealand and today provides the norm for juvenile justice in that country. Because this model is less well-known than other forms, at least in the United States, I will describe it somewhat more thoroughly than the others.

Responding to a crisis in the welfare and justice system for juveniles, and criticized by the indigenous Maori population for utilizing an imposed, alien, colonial system, New Zealand revolutionized its juvenile justice system in 1989. While the court system remains as a backup, the intended "default" response to most serious juvenile crime in New Zealand today is an FGC.[3]

Consequently, family group conferences can be seen as both a system of justice and as a mode of encounter in New Zealand.

Conferences are put together and facilitated by paid social service personnel called youth justice coordinators. It is their job to help families determine who should be present and to design the process that will be appropriate for them. One of the goals of the process is to be culturally appropriate, and the form of the conference is supposed to be adapted to the needs and cultures of all involved.

This is not a scripted model of facilitation. While there is often a common overall progression in the conferences, each is adapted to the needs of its particular parties. An element common to most conferences is a family caucus sometime during the conference. Here the one who has offended and her or his family go to another room to discuss what has happened and to develop a proposal to bring back to those who have been harmed and the rest of the conference.

Like the facilitator in a VOC, the coordinator of a FGC must seek to be impartial, or perhaps more accurately, equally partial to both sides, balancing the concerns and interests of all. However, he or she is charged with making sure a plan is developed that addresses causes as well as reparation, that holds the offender adequately accountable, and that is realistic.

While the community is not explicitly included, these conferences are more inclusive than VOCs. Family members of the offending person are an essential part and play very important roles—indeed, this is seen as a family empowerment model. Those who have been victimized may bring family members or victim advocates. A special attorney or youth advocate may be present, and other caregivers may be as well. In addition, since the police play a prosecutorial role in New Zealand, they must be represented.

Family group conferences, New Zealand style, are not designed simply to allow for the expression of facts and feelings and to develop restitution agreements. Because they normally take the place of a court, they are charged with developing the entire plan for the young person who offended that, in addition to reparations, includes elements of prevention and sometimes punishment. Even the actual charges may be negotiated in this meeting. Interestingly, the plan is intended to be the consensus of everyone in the confer-

> **New Zealand FGCs address both reparation and prevention.**

ence. The victim, the offender, or the police can each block an outcome if one of them is unsatisfied.

Family group conferences, then, enlarge the circle of participants to include family members or other significant people and perhaps justice officials as well. At least in the New Zealand form, a conference involves a family caucus, and the facilitator may have an enlarged role compared to a VOC, making sure that the person who caused the harm is being held appropriately accountable. FGCs, sometimes called community or accountability conferences, are being adapted in a number of countries. They also provide the framework for some of the pre-charge diversion programs within the U.S., though the actual conference may be conducted as a circle process, described below.

Circles

Circle approaches entered the restorative justice field initially from Aboriginal communities in Canada. Judge Barry Stuart, in whose court a circle was first acknowledged in a legal ruling, has chosen the term "peacemaking circles" to describe this form. Today, circles are being used for many purposes. In addition to sentencing circles, intended to determine sentences in criminal cases, there are healing circles, circles to deal with workplace conflicts, even circles designed as forms of community dialogue.

In a circle process, participants arrange themselves in a circle. They pass a "talking piece" around the circle to assure that each person speaks, one at a time, in the order in which each is seated in the circle. One or two "circle keepers" serve as facilitators of the circle. In indigenous communities, elders play an important role in leading the circle or in offering advice and insight.

A set of values, or even a philosophy, is often articulated as part of the process—values that emphasize respect, the value of each participant, integrity, the importance of speaking from the heart, and so on.

Circles consciously enlarge the circle of participants. Those who have been harmed, those who have caused harm, their family members, and sometimes justice officials are included, but community members are essential participants as well. Sometimes these community members are invited because of their connection to or interest in the specific offense or the parties involved; sometimes they are part of an ongoing circle of volunteers from the community.

Because the community is involved, discussions within the circle are often more wide-ranging than in other restorative justice models. Participants may address situations in the community that are giving rise to the offense, the support needs of both those who have experienced and caused harm, the obligations that the community might have, community norms, or other related community issues.

Although circles initially emerged from small, homogeneous communities, they are today being used in a variety of communities, including large urban areas, and for a variety of situations besides criminal cases. Circles seem to be the predominant model in educational settings. Indeed, circle processes appear to be the closest thing to a "universal" model of addressing harm and conflict that I have seen. My graduate students, who come from many countries and traditions, often note that circles are or were used in their traditions.

Circles have wide application.

This is not the place to discuss the many forms or the relative merits of each restorative justice model. What should be noted here is that all of the above are forms of encounter. They can be differentiated, however, by the numbers and categories of stakeholders who are included and by their somewhat different styles of facilitation.

Again, these forms are increasingly being blended so that the differences among them seem less significant than before.

Please note that not all restorative approaches involve a direct encounter, and not all needs can be met through an encounter. While those who have been victimized have some needs that involve the person who harmed them, they also have needs that do not. Similarly, those

> **Restorative justice may not involve an encounter.**

who offend have needs and obligations that are not directly connected to those they have harmed. Thus the following typology includes both encounter and non-encounter programs.

Models differ in their goals

Another way to understand the differences between these various approaches in a criminal justice context is to examine their goals. These can be placed in three categories, though they often overlap.

Alternative or diversionary programs

These programs usually aim to divert cases from, or provide an alternative to, all or some part of the criminal justice process or sentencing. Police or prosecutors may make a referral, deferring prosecution and ultimately dropping it if the case is satisfactorily settled. A judge may refer a case to a restorative conference to sort out elements of the sentence, such as restitution. In some circle processes, the prosecutor and judge may join the community in a circle designed to develop a sentence tailored to the needs of the victim, offender, and community. In Batavia, New York, a long-standing restorative justice program has worked first with victims of severe crime, then with offenders, to develop alternative pleas, sentences, and even sometimes bail agreements. In New Zealand, of course, conferences are the norm, and courts are the alternative. Pre-charge diversion programs such as those in Oakland, California, and Concord, Massachusetts, seek to keep young people out of the system by holding the offending person accountable, addressing the environment that has contributed to the offending behavior, and meeting the needs of those who were harmed.

Healing or therapeutic programs

Increasingly, restorative programs, such as victim offender dialogue conferences, are being developed for the most severe kinds of crimes—violent assault, even rape and murder. Often the offending party in these situations is in prison. In such encounter programs, involvement is not usually designed to impact the outcome of the case. With appropriate preparation and structure, such encounters have been found to be powerful, positive experiences for both victims and offenders, regardless of who initiates them.

Not all programs in this category involve direct encounters between victims and offenders from the same incident. For example, when the person who has caused the harm is not available, or the person harmed is not ready to meet with him or her, it can be helpful for the person harmed to meet with a surrogate offender who has caused a similar harm. Or an offender may meet with a surrogate victim.

Some such programs function as a form of victim-oriented offender rehabilitation. As part of the treatment process, those who have offended are encouraged to understand and take responsibility for what they have done. Victim-impact panels, where groups of victims are given an opportunity to tell their stories to offenders, may be part of this process.

Other programs such as Bridges to Life offer multiple-session, in-prison seminars that bring victims and offenders not involved in the same case, and sometimes community members, together to explore a variety of topics and issues, for the benefit of all involved.

Transitional programs

A growing area of restorative programming has to do with transitions after prison. In both halfway houses and in prisons, programs are being designed around victim harm and offender accountability in order to help both victims and offenders as the offender returns to the community.

One model is the Circles of Support and Accountability (CSA or CoSA) developed in Canada to work with men who had committed sex offenses and were being released from prison. In much of the U.S. and Canada, those who have committed such offenses and have served their sentences are released into communities with little support for the former prisoner and with great fear from the community and those they have victimized. These individuals are often ostracized by the communities that know them best, so they move on to other communities where they are not known. Given this, their rates of recidivism can be high.

Circles of Support and Accountability gather a circle of people—former prisoners, community members, even victims of similar offenses—not only to support the person who has offended, but also to hold them accountable. Initially the interaction is intense with daily check-ins and strict guidelines for what the person can do and where the person can go. Working with the ex-prisoners to take responsibility for their behavior, while putting necessary support in place, these circles have been successful in reintegrating former prisoners while allaying community fears. This model has now expanded beyond sex offenses and is increasingly being used for prisoner re-entry generally and has been found to reduce repeat offending.

Increasingly people in prison are taking the initiative to establish restorative justice groups and/or trainings within prison, and these do not easily fit into the three categories above. Prisoners at Graterford prison in Pennsylvania, for example, have developed their own training curriculum that is used to help their peers understand and address their behavior and its consequences. In the near future they hope to take this training approach national, making it available to others. *The Little Book of Restorative Justice for People in Prison* reflects the general philosophy and approach behind this.[4]

So although the "core" restorative justice programs involve direct encounters between those harmed and those causing harm, a variety of approaches are less direct. In order to make sense of all these forms, a continuum may be helpful.

A restorative continuum

In theory, most circle or conferencing models providing a direct encounter between those harmed and those causing harm would be considered fully restorative. Conducted properly, consistent with the principles and values of restorative justice, they meet all of the criteria laid out in the guidelines for restorative justice that I outlined earlier. But what about other approaches that claim to be restorative? What about those that don't involve a direct encounter? Are there other options within the restorative framework?

It is important to view restorative justice models along a continuum, from fully restorative to not restorative, with several points or categories in between.

Seven key questions help to analyze both the effectiveness and the extent of restorative justice models for particular situations.

Degrees of restorative justice practices: a continuum

fully restorative	mostly restorative	partially restorative	potentially restorative	pseudo- or non-restorative

1. Does the model address harms, needs, and causes for all involved?

2. Is it adequately oriented to the needs of those who have been harmed?

3. Are those who offended encouraged to take responsibility?

4. Are all relevant stakeholders involved?

5. Is there an opportunity for dialogue and participatory decision-making?

6. Is the model respectful to all parties?

7. Does the model treat all equally, maintaining awareness of and addressing imbalances of power?

While conferencing or encounter programs may be fully restorative, there are situations in which these models do not fully—or even partially—apply. What about victims in cases where offenders are not apprehended or offenders are unwilling to take responsibility?

In a restorative system, services would start immediately after a crime to address victim needs and to involve the victim, regardless of whether an offender is apprehended. Thus victim assistance, while it cannot be seen as fully restorative, is an important component of a restorative system and should be seen at least as partially restorative.

> **Restorative options are important for victims, regardless of whether an offender is identified.**

Victim impact panels, without matching victims and offenders from a specific case, allow those who experienced harm to tell their stories and encourage those who have caused harm to understand what they have done. These are an important part of a restorative approach and can be seen as partly or mostly restorative.

Similarly, what happens when someone who has offended is willing to take steps to understand and to take responsibility, but the person or persons they harmed are unavailable or unwilling? A few programs for such circumstances have been developed (such as offering opportunities to learn from those harmed and to do symbolic acts of restitution), but more should be available. While perhaps not fully restorative, these programs play an essential role in the overall system of justice.

Do offender treatment or rehabilitation programs qualify as restorative justice practices? Treatment for those who have offended can be seen as a part of prevention and, along with prisoner reintegration, has some kinship with restorative justice. However, as conventionally practiced, many efforts at treatment or rehabilitation offer little that is explicitly restorative. They could, however, function restoratively, and some do by organizing treatment around helping those who have caused harm to understand and take responsibility for it and, at the same time, giving as much attention as possible to the needs of those who have been harmed.

Depending on how it is done, offender treatment may fall into the "potentially" or "partially" categories.

Community service may or may not be restorative.

Similarly, offender advocacy, prisoner re-entry programs, or religious teaching in prison are in themselves not restorative; however, they may play an important role in a restorative system, especially if they are reshaped to include a restorative framework.

In my view, community service falls into the "potentially restorative" category. As currently practiced, community service is at best an alternative form of punishment, not restorative justice. In New Zealand, however, community service often is part of the outcome of a family group conference. All in the group have participated in developing the plan, the work is connected to the offense as much as possible, and within the plan are specifics about how the community and family will support and monitor the agreement. Here it has potential for being seen as repayment or a contribution to the community, mutually agreed upon by all participants. With this kind of re-framing, community service may have an important place in a restorative approach.

Then there is the "pseudo-" or "non-restorative" category. "Restorative" has become such a popular term that many acts and efforts are being labeled "restorative," but in fact they are not. Some of these might be rescued. Others cannot. The death penalty, which causes additional and irreparable harm, is one of the latter.

CHAPTER 4

Where from Here?

In my earlier writings, I often drew a sharp contrast between the retributive framework of the legal or criminal justice system and a more restorative approach to justice. Later, however, I came to realize that this polarization can be somewhat misleading. Although charts that highlight contrasting characteristics illuminate important elements differentiating the two approaches, they also hide important similarities and areas of collaboration.

Retributive justice vs. restorative justice

Philosopher of law Conrad Brunk has argued that on the theoretical or philosophical level, retribution and restoration are not the polar opposites that we often assume.[1] In fact, they have much in common. A primary goal of both retributive theory and restorative theory is to vindicate through reciprocity, by "balancing the scales." Where they differ is in what each suggests will effectively right the balance.

Both retributive and restorative theories of justice acknowledge a basic moral intuition that a balance has been thrown off by a wrongdoing. Consequently, the victim deserves something and the offender owes something. Both argue that the person who offends must be treated as a moral agent. Both approaches argue that there must be a proportional relationship between the act and the response.

> **Retribution and restoration share a concern for balance.**

They differ, however, on the currency that will fulfill the obligations and right the balance.

Retributive theory believes that pain will vindicate, but in practice that is often counterproductive for both the one harmed and the one causing harm. Restorative justice theory, on the other hand, argues that what truly vindicates is acknowledgment of a victim's harms and needs, combined with an active effort to encourage the offender to take responsibility, make right the wrongs, and address the causes of his or her behavior. By addressing this need for vindication in a positive way, restorative justice has the potential to affirm all parties and to help them transform their lives.

Criminal justice vs. restorative justice

Restorative justice advocates dream of a day when justice is fully restorative. Whether this is realistic is debatable, at least in the immediate future. More attainable, perhaps, is a time when restorative justice processes are the norm, while some form of the legal or criminal justice system provides the backup or alternative. Ideally, though, that backup system would be guided by restorative principles and values as well.

Society must have a system to sort out the "truth" as best it can when people deny responsibility. Some cases are simply too difficult or horrendous to be worked out by those with a direct stake in the offense. Some people involved in certain cases may choose to not be a part of working out the outcome. We must have a process that gives attention to those societal needs and obligations that go beyond the ones held by the immediate stakeholders. We also must not lose those qualities that the legal system, when operating properly, represents: the rule of law, due process, a deep regard for human rights, the orderly development of law.

A goal: be as restorative as possible.

Justice might be viewed as a continuum. On the one end is the Western legal or criminal justice system model. Its strengths—such as the encouragement of human rights—are substantial. Yet it has some glaring weaknesses. At the other end is the restorative alternative. It, too, has important strengths. It, too, has limits, at least as it is currently conceived and practiced.

A realistic goal, perhaps, is to move as far as we can toward an approach that is restorative. In some cases or situations, we may not be able to move very far. In others, we may achieve processes and outcomes that are truly restorative. In between will be many cases and situations where both systems must be utilized, and justice is only partly restorative.[2] Meanwhile, we can dream of a day when this particular continuum is no longer relevant because all will rest on a restorative foundation.

One vision

In my own dreams, a truly restorative justice approach would involve true cooperation between communities and the justice system. We would use collaborative community-based restorative processes to keep people out of the formal system whenever possible. Within the system, lawyers (including prosecutors) would envision themselves less as gladiators out to win than as healers and problem-solvers; as Doug Noll has suggested, their job would be not only to lay out the legal options but to provide clients with a "conflict map" of the situation and the non-legal options.[3] Susan Herman has suggested that a "parallel justice" system should be available for those who are victimized, regardless of whether the offending party has been identified, helping those harmed to define and meet their needs. A parallel system could offer restorative interactions with those who have offended where desired and possible.[4] A truly independent victim assistance office would be trusted by both prosecution and defense and thus able to obtain the information victims need from both sides. Everyone in the system—from law enforcement to judges and beyond—would be asking the restorative justice questions such as these: Who has been harmed? What are their needs? Whose obligations are they? The adversarial court system and prison would be used as last resorts and would be operated on restorative principles and values as much as possible.[5] Due process protections would be built in, but in a non-adversarial manner. Everyone involved would seek to base their actions on a clear set of restorative principles and values, and outcomes would be assessed by these standards.

But that is just one dream, undoubtedly limited and flawed by my own "lens." To envision what a truly restorative "system" or approach might look like will require dialogue among many and diverse voices. As Dutch law professor Herman Bianchi used to say to the newly-developing restorative justice movement, true justice requires endless "palaver."

True justice requires ongoing dialogue.

Dreams and visions are important. As I said in the Afterward to *Changing Lenses*,[6]

> I believe in ideals. Much of the time we fall short of them, but they remain a beacon, something toward which to aim, something against which to test our actions. They point a direction. Only with a sense of direction can we know when we are off the path.

And my last paragraph of the Afterward, and of the book, was this:

> My hope is that you will understand this as a vision—a vision that is less an elusive mirage than it is an indistinct destination on a necessarily long and circuitous road.

A way of life

During the years I have been involved in this work, many people have commented that restorative justice is in fact a way of life. At first I was mystified; how can an approach designed initially to respond to crime become a life philosophy? I have concluded that it has to do with the ethical system that restorative justice embodies.

The Western criminal justice system is intended to promote important positive values—a recognition of the rights of others, the importance of certain boundaries on behavior, the centrality of human rights. But it does so in a way that is largely negative; it says that if you harm others, we will harm you. As James Gilligan has argued, it is a mirror image of the offending act.[7] Consequently, to make it humane, we have to bring in other values to govern and mitigate it. It does not, in itself, offer us a vision of the good.

Restorative justice, on the other hand, provides an inherently positive value system, a vision of how we can live together in a life-giving way. It is based on the assumption—a reminder for those of us living in an individualistic world—that we are interconnected. It reminds us that we live in relationship, that our actions impact others, that when those actions are harmful we have responsibilities.

As I noted earlier, restorative justice must be grounded in values. Many values can and have been articulated, but I like to focus on three "R" values: respect, responsibility, and relationship. The last one is foundational. It reminds us of a basic reality, one that is understood clearly in most religious and cultural traditions. It is also a foundational aspect of human nature; as Daniel

Goleman has pointed out, neuroscience is finding that we as human beings are "wired to connect" with others.[8]

Restorative justice is a river

Years ago, while living in Pennsylvania, my wife and I set out to find the source of the Susquehanna River that flows through that state. We followed one of its two branches until we arrived behind a farmer's barn and found a rusty pipe sticking out of a hill. Fed by a spring, the water fell from the pipe into a bathtub that served as a watering trough for cattle. It spilled over the bathtub, spread out along the ground, then formed the stream that eventually became a mighty river.

It is, of course, debatable whether this particular spring is *the* source. There are other springs in the vicinity that could compete for that honor. And, of course, this stream would not be a river if it were not fed by hundreds of other streams. Nevertheless, this river and this spring have become my metaphor for the restorative justice movement.

The contemporary field of restorative justice started as a tiny trickle in the 1970s, an effort by a handful of people dreaming of doing justice differently. It originated in practice and in experimentation rather than in abstractions. The theory, the concept, came later. But while the immediate sources of the modern restorative justice stream are recent, both concept and practice draw upon traditions as deep as human history and as wide as the world community.

For some time, the restorative justice stream was driven underground by our modern legal systems. In recent decades, however, that stream has resurfaced, growing into a widening river. Restorative justice today is acknowledged worldwide by governments and communities concerned about crime. Thousands of people around the globe bring their experience and expertise to the river. This river, like all rivers, exists because it is fed by numerous tributaries flowing in from around the world.

Some of the feeder streams are practical programs, such as those being implemented in many countries. The river is also being fed by a variety of indigenous traditions and current adaptations which draw upon those traditions: family group conferences inspired by Maori traditions in New Zealand, for example; sentencing circles from First Nation communities in the Canadian North; Navajo peacemaking courts; African customary law; or the Afghani practice of *jirga*. The field of mediation and conflict resolution feeds into that river, as do the victim rights and assistance movements and alternatives-to-prison movements of the past decades. A variety of religious traditions flow into this river.

While the experiments, practices, and customs from many communities and cultures are instructive, none can or should be copied and simply plugged into other communities or societies. Rather, they should be viewed as examples of how different communities and societies found their own appropriate

> Justice processes must be context-appropriate.

ways to express justice as a response to wrongdoing. These approaches may give us inspiration and a place to begin. While these examples and traditions may not provide blueprints, they may serve as catalysts for forming ideas and directions.

This context-oriented approach to justice reminds us that true justice emerges from conversation and takes into account local needs and traditions. This is one of the reasons why we must be very cautious about top-down strategies for implementing restorative justice.

The argument presented here is quite simple. Justice will not be served if we maintain our exclusive focus on the questions that drive our current justice systems: What laws have been broken? Who did it? What do they deserve?

True justice requires, instead, that we ask questions such as these: Who has been hurt? What do they need? Whose obligations and responsibilities are these? Who has a stake in this situation? What are the causes that have contributed to this? What is the process that can involve the stakeholders in finding a solution? Restorative justice requires us to change not just our lenses but also our questions.

Above all, restorative justice is an invitation to join in conversation so that we may support and learn from each other. It is a reminder that all of us are indeed embedded in a web of relationships.

Fundamental Principles of Restorative Justice

Howard Zehr and Harry Mika[1]

*These principles, first published in 1998, are in some ways
dated. For the sake of continuity, however we have decided to
reproduce them in their original form. We encourage you
to update and adapt them to your situation.*

1.0 Crime is fundamentally a violation of people and interpersonal relationships.

1.1 Victims and the community have been harmed and are in need of restoration.

1.1.1 The primary victims are those most directly affected by the offense, but others, such as family members of victims and offenders, witnesses, and members of the affected community, are also victims.

1.1.2 The relationships affected (and reflected) by crime must be addressed.

1.1.3 Restoration is a continuum of responses to the range of needs and harms experienced by victims, offenders, and the community.

1.2 Victims, offenders, and the affected communities are the key stakeholders in justice.

1.2.1 A restorative justice process maximizes the input and participation of these parties—but especially primary victims as well as offenders—in the search for restoration, healing, responsibility, and prevention.

1.2.2 The roles of these parties will vary according to the nature of the offense, as well as the capacities and preferences of the parties.

1.2.3 The state has circumscribed roles, such as investigating facts, facilitating processes, and ensuring safety, but the state is not a primary victim.

2.0 Violations create obligations and liabilities.

2.1 Offenders' obligations are to make things right as much as possible.

2.1.1 Since the primary obligation is to victims, a restorative justice process empowers victims to effectively participate in defining obligations.

2.1.2 Offenders are provided opportunities and encouragement to understand the harm they have caused to victims and the community and to develop plans for taking appropriate responsibility.

2.1.3 Voluntary participation by offenders is maximized; coercion and exclusion are minimized. However, offenders may be required to accept their obligations if they do not do so voluntarily.

2.1.4 Obligations that follow from the harm inflicted by crime should be related to making things right.

2.1.5 Obligations may be experienced as difficult, even painful, but are not intended as pain, vengeance, or revenge.

2.1.6 Obligations to victims, such as restitution, take priority over other sanctions and obligations to the state, such as fines.

2.1.7 Offenders have an obligation to be active participants in addressing their own needs.

2.2 *The community's obligations are to victims and to offenders and for the general welfare of its members.*

2.2.1 The community has a responsibility to support and help victims of crime to meet their needs.

2.2.2 The community bears a responsibility for the welfare of its members and the social conditions and relationships that promote both crime and community peace.

2.2.3 The community has responsibilities to support efforts to integrate offenders into the community, to be actively involved in the definitions of offender obligations, and to ensure opportunities for offenders to make amends.

3.0 Restorative justice seeks to heal and put right the wrongs.

3.1 *The needs of victims for information, validation, vindication, restitution, testimony, safety, and support are the starting points of justice.*

3.1.1 The safety of victims is an immediate priority.

3.1.2 The justice process provides a framework that promotes the work of recovery and healing that is ultimately the domain of the individual victim.

3.1.3 Victims are empowered by maximizing their input and by participation in determining needs and outcomes.

3.1.4 Offenders are involved in repair of the harm insofar as possible.

3.2 The process of justice maximizes opportunities for exchange of information, participation, dialogue, and mutual consent between victim and offender.

3.2.1 Face-to-face encounters are appropriate in some instances, while alternative forms of exchange are more appropriate in others.

3.2.2 Victims have the principal role in defining and directing the terms and conditions of the exchange.

3.2.3 Mutual agreement takes precedence over imposed outcomes.

3.2.4 Opportunities are provided for remorse, forgiveness, and reconciliation.

3.3 Offenders' needs and competencies are addressed.

3.3.1 Recognizing that offenders themselves have often been harmed, healing and integration of offenders into the community are emphasized.

3.3.2 Offenders are supported and treated respectfully in the justice process.

3.3.3 Removal from the community and severe restriction of offenders is limited to the minimum necessary.

3.3.4 Justice values personal change above compliant behavior.

3.4 *The justice process belongs to the community.*

3.4.1 Community members are actively involved in doing justice.

3.4.2 The justice process draws from community resources and, in turn, contributes to the building and strengthening of community.

3.4.3 The justice process attempts to promote changes in the community to both prevent similar harms from happening to others, and to foster early intervention to address the needs of victims and the accountability of offenders.

3.5 *Justice is mindful of the outcomes, intended and unintended, of its responses to crime and victimization.*

3.5.1 Justice monitors and encourages follow-through since healing, recovery, accountability, and change are maximized when agreements are kept.

3.5.2 Fairness is assured, not by uniformity of outcomes, but through provision of necessary support and opportunities to all parties as well as avoidance of discrimination based on ethnicity, class, and sex.

3.5.3 Outcomes that are predominately deterrent or incapacitative should be implemented as a last resort, involving the least restrictive intervention while seeking restoration of the parties involved.

3.5.4 Unintended consequences, such as the cooptation of restorative processes for coercive or punitive ends, undue offender orientation, or the expansion of social control, are resisted.

Note: *Appendix II is a resource that may be useful to the reader or for use in discussions or presentations. It may be reproduced with proper citation.*

APPENDIX II

Restorative Justice in Threes

Howard Zehr

3 assumptions underlie restorative justice:

- When people and relationships are harmed, needs are created;
- The needs created by harms lead to obligations;
- The obligation is to heal and "put right" the harms; this is a just response.

3 principles of restorative justice reflect these assumptions. A just response:

- Repairs the harm caused by, and revealed by, wrongdoing (restoration);
- Encourages appropriate responsibility for addressing needs and repairing the harm (accountability);
- Involves those impacted, including the community, in the resolution (engagement).

3 underlying *values* provide the foundation:
- Respect;
- Responsibility;
- Relationship.

3 *questions* are central to restorative justice:
- Who has been hurt?
- What are their needs?
- Who has the obligation to address the needs, to put right the harms, to restore relationships?

(As opposed to: What rules were broken? Who did it? What do they deserve?)

3 *stakeholder* groups should be considered and/or involved:
- Those who have been harmed, and their families;
- Those who have caused harm, and their families;
- The relevant community or communities.

3 *aspirations* guide restorative justice: the desire to live in right relationship:
- With one another;
- With the creation;
- With the creator.

Note: *Appendix III is a resource that may be useful to the reader or for use in discussions or presentations. It may be reproduced with proper citation.*

APPENDIX III

Restorative Justice? What's That?

Howard Zehr

D o a Google search for the phrase "restorative justice," and you will get over a million hits—and this for a term that was virtually non-existent 35 years ago. Ask what it means, and you may get a variety of answers.

For many, it implies a meeting between victims of crime and those who have committed those crimes. A family meets with the teenagers who burglarized their home, expressing their feelings and negotiating a plan for repayment. Parents meet with the man who murdered their daughter to tell him the impact and get answers to their questions. A school principal and his family meet with the boys who exploded a pipe bomb in their front yard, narrowly missing the principal and his infant child. The family's and the neighbors' fears of a recurrence are put to rest, and the boys for the first time understand the enormity of what they have done.

Restorative justice does include encounter programs for those harmed and those causing harm; today there are thousands of such programs all over the world. But restorative justice is more than an encounter, and its scope reaches far beyond the criminal justice system. Increasingly schools are implementing restorative disciplinary processes, religious bodies are using restorative approaches to deal with wrongdoing—including clergy sexual abuse—and whole societies are considering restorative approaches to address wrongs done on a mass scale. Of growing popularity are restorative conferences or circle processes that bring groups of people together to share perspectives and concerns and collaboratively find solutions to the problems facing their families and communities.

Restorative justice emerged in the 1970s as an effort to correct some of the weaknesses of the Western legal system while building on its strengths. An area of special concern has been the neglect of victims and their needs; legal justice is largely about what to do with offenders. It has also been driven by a desire to hold those who cause harm truly accountable. Recognizing that punishment is often ineffective, restorative justice aims at helping those who offend to recognize the harm they have caused and encouraging them to repair the harm, to the extent it is possible. Rather than obsessing about whether those who offend get what they deserve, restorative justice focuses on repairing the harm of crime and engaging individuals and community members in the process.

It is basically common sense—the kind of lessons our parents and fore-parents taught—and that has led some to call it a way of life. When a wrong has been done, it needs to be named and acknowledged. Those who have been harmed need to be able to grieve their losses, to be able to tell their stories, to have their questions answered—that is, to have the harms and needs caused by the offense addressed. They—and we—need to have those who have done wrong accept their responsibility and take steps to repair the harm to the extent it is possible.

As you might imagine with so many Google references, the usage of the term varies widely. Sometimes it is used in ways that are rather far removed from what those in the field have intended. So when you see the term, you might ask yourself these questions: Are the wrongs being acknowledged? Are the needs of those who were harmed being addressed? Is the one who committed the harm being encouraged to understand the damage and accept his or her obligation to make right the wrong? Are those involved in or affected by this being invited to be part of the "solution"? Is concern being shown for everyone involved? If the answers to these questions are "no," then even though it may have restorative elements, it isn't restorative justice.

Note: *Appendix IV is a resource that may be useful to the reader or for use in discussions or presentations. It may be reproduced with proper citation.*

APPENDIX IV

Ten Ways to Live Restoratively

Howard Zehr[1]

1. Take relationships seriously, envisioning yourself in an interconnected web of people, institutions, and the environment.

2. Try to be aware of the impact—potential as well as actual—of your actions on others and the environment.

3. When your actions negatively impact others, take responsibility by acknowledging and seeking to repair the harm—even when you could probably get away with avoiding or denying it.

4. Treat everyone respectfully, even those you don't expect to encounter again, even those you feel don't deserve it, even those who have harmed or offended you or others.

5. Involve those affected by a decision, as much as possible, in the decision-making process.

6. View the conflicts and harms in your life as opportunities.

7. Listen, deeply and compassionately, to others, seeking to understand even if you don't agree with them. (Think about who you want to be in the latter situation rather than just being right.)

8. Engage in dialogue with others, even when what is being said is difficult, remaining open to learning from them and the encounter.

9. Be cautious about imposing your "truths" and views on other people and situations.

10. Sensitively confront everyday injustices including sexism, racism, homophobia, and classism.

The chart below explores some implications of five key restorative justice principles for criminal justice and for restorative living.

Restorative Justice Principles adapted by Catherine Bargen from Susan Sharpe, *Restorative Justice: A Vision for Healing and Change*. Thanks to Catherine for her suggestions on the above as well.

Ten Ways to Live Restoratively

Principle of Restorative Justice	Application for Criminal Justice	Application for Restorative Living
Invite full participation and consensus.	Victims, offenders, and the community have a voice in responding to criminal harm, with as much agreement as possible in what the outcome should look like.	All those who feel they have a stake in a situation of harm or conflict can be invited to participate in dialogue around the issues and have a voice in the outcomes or decisions made. Power imbalances are noted and addressed as much as possible to achieve consensus.
Heal what has been broken.	When a crime is committed, the need for healing inevitably arises. This may take the form of emotional healing (for victims and for offenders), relationship healing, and/or reparation of property damage.	Our everyday interactions and situations can result in hurtful words and actions, which may create feelings of injustice or imbalance in our relationships. As much as possible, the restorative approach seeks to bring those hurts to light and create space for healing and reparation.
Seek full and direct accountability.	Offenders need to take responsibility for their own actions and choices. They are given the opportunity to explain their behavior and fulfill the obligations created from their behavior directly to the people they have harmed.	When harm occurs, we can nurture an environment where we are encouraged to take ownership for our own roles in hurtful behavior or abuses of power. Living restoratively means respectfully expecting oneself and others to be accountable for our actions in ways that are fair and reasonable.

Principle of Restorative Justice	Application for Criminal Justice	Application for Restorative Living
Reunite what has been divided.	Victims of crime often experience a sense of isolation from the community, as do offenders. While the reasons for this isolation may differ between these two groups, processes that allow for reintegration need to be sought in the wake of a crime for all that have been affected. Such processes can create a renewed sense of wholeness and "closure," as well as a sense of reintegration into the community.	Hurtful or damaging behavior in our places of interaction can create feelings of isolation and of being an outcast. It can result in individuals taking sides and developing an "us/them" mentality. As much as possible, restorative living aims to take stock of where divisions have occurred in our communities and to work toward balance, understanding, and reconciliation.
Strengthen the community to prevent future harms.	A justice process that is restorative will focus not only on the details of the crime at hand, but what the systemic causes of crime are in the community and how they can be addressed. In this way, a healthier and safer community is created for all, not just those wanting to be protected from crime.	Most communities can ultimately use situations of harm to learn, grow, and change where necessary. When living restoratively, we can help illuminate systemic injustice and power imbalances. We then advocate for positive changes in order to make the community a healthier and more just place for all.

Restorative Justice and Peacebuilding

At the Center for Justice and Peacebuilding, where I am on the faculty, we envision the peacebuilding field as a broad umbrella term. As my colleague Lisa Schirch explains in *The Little Book of Strategic Peacebuilding* (Good Books, 2004), it encompasses a wide range of fields, programs, and approaches aimed at creating a just and peaceful society.

One way of defining peacebuilding is that it is about building and maintaining healthy relationships and mending those that have been broken. Given that focus, restorative justice can be viewed as adding the following specific contributions to peacebuilding and to fields within peacebuilding such as conflict resolution or transformation:

1. Recognition that conflict involves injustices that must be addressed;

2. A relational understanding of wrongdoing that focuses on the impact on people and relationships rather than rules;

3. A set of principles to guide us when a harm or wrong has occurred;

4. A group of specific practices that, although they use some skill sets similar to those for conflict resolution, allow participants to name and address the harms involved and the resulting obligations;

5. An explicit grounding in core values and principles that guide the process and are fundamental for healthy relationships.

ENDNOTES

Chapter 1

[1] Howard Zehr, *Transcending: Reflections of Crime Victims* (Good Books, 2001), 9.

[2] A fuller treatment of the justice needs of victims may be found in Zehr, *Transcending: Reflections of Crime Victims*, Part 2.

[3] Shame theory has emerged as an important topic in restorative justice. In his pioneering book, *Crime, shame and reintegration* (Cambridge University Press, 1989), John Braithwaite argues that shame that stigmatizes pushes people toward crime. Shame may be "re-integrative," however, when it denounces the offense but not the offender and opportunities are provided for the shame to be removed or transformed. The topic is highly controversial, however, and the best research suggests that shame is indeed a factor in both victimization and offending, but it has to be handled very carefully. In most situations, the focus needs to be on managing or transforming shame rather than imposing it.

[4] See Carolyn Yoder, *The Little Book of Trauma Healing* (Good Books, 2005).

[5] See Kay Pranis, *The Little Book of Circle Processes* (Good Books, 2005), and Kay Pranis, Barry Stuart, and Mark Wedge, *Peacemaking Circles: From Crime to Community* (Living Justice Press, 2003).

Chapter 2

[1] See http://emu.edu/now/restorative-justice/, May 2, 2013 as well as Ross London, *Crime, Punishment, and Restorative Justice: From the Margins to the Mainstream* (Lynne Rienner Publishers, 2010).

[2] An overview of this debate may be found in Gerry Johnstone, *Restorative Justice: Ideas, Values, Debates* (Willan, 2002), 136ff. This book provides a helpful overview and analysis of the debates and critical issues in the field of restorative justice.

[3] The role of the state is most contested in situations where minority groups have felt systematically oppressed by the government (e.g., in Northern Ireland or much of urban America) or where the state is viewed as having coopted restorative justice while implementing it from the top down. The latter has been a particular concern of community and indigenous groups, for example, in New Zealand and Canada.

[4] James Gilligan, *Violence: Reflections on a National Epidemic* (Random House, 1996).

[5] Sandra Bloom, *Creating Sanctuary: Toward the Evolution of Sane Societies* (Routledge, 1997). See also Carolyn Yoder, *The Little Book of Trauma Healing* (Good Books, 2005).

[6] Jarem Sawatsky, *Justpeace Ethics: A Guide to Restorative Justice and Peacebuilding* (Cascade Books, 2009).

[7] This is an adaptation of Tony Marshall's widely cited definition: "Restorative justice is a process whereby all parties with a stake in a specific offense come together to resolve collectively how to deal with the aftermath of the offense and its implications for the future."

[8] Susan Sharpe, *Restorative Justice: A Vision for Healing and Change* (Edmonton, Alberta: Mediation and Restorative Justice Centre, 1998).

[9] The word "closure" is often offensive to victims, especially victims of severe crime. It seems to suggest that all can be put behind and the book closed, and that is not possible.

However, the word also implies a sense of being able to move forward, which restorative justice aims to make possible.

[10] These signposts were originally published, in a somewhat different version, as a bookmark by Mennonite Central Committee, Akron, Pennsylvania, in 1997. I have made slight modifications in this edition.

Chapter 3

[1] See http://peace.fresno.edu/docs/APeacemakingModel.pdf.

[2] See http://www.nytimes.com/2013/01/06/magazine/can-forgiveness-play-a-role-in-criminal-justice.html.

[3] The youth justice system in New Zealand is designed to divert offenders in less serious cases out of the system, avoiding both a formal FGC and court. (This is sometimes done in conjunction with an informal victim offender conference.) This design is based on the assumptions that much youth offending is part of a developmental stage and that entering youth into the formal system may encourage future offending behavior.

[4] Barb Toews, *The Little Book of Restorative Justice for People in Prison* (Good Books, 2006).

Chapter 4

[1] Conrad Brunk, "Restorative Justice and the Philosophical Theories of Criminal Punishment" in *The Spiritual Roots of Restorative Justice,* Michael L. Hadley, editor (State University of New York Press, 2001), 31-56.

[2] In *Restorative Justice and Responsive Regulation* (Oxford University Press, 2002), John Braithwaite suggests an interesting model for how restoration, deterrence, and incapacitation might be addressed in restorative justice.

[3] Doug Noll, *Peacemaking: Practicing at the Intersection of Law and Human Conflict* (Cascadia, 2003).

[4] Susan Herman, *Parallel Justice for Victims of Crime* (National Center for Victims of Crime, 2010).

[5] For example, in *The Legacy of Community Justice*, edited by Sandra Pavelka, Anne Seymour, and Barry Stuart (Vernon, British Columbia: JCharlton Publishing Ltd, 2013), Dennis Maloney, Gordon Bazemore, and Joe Hudson outline the way probation might be reshaped so that probation officers become "community justice officers" who facilitate community responses to crime and mobilize community resources. Also of interest is Judge Fred McElrea's chapter, "Restorative Justice as a Procedural Revolution: Some Lessons from the Adversary System" in *Civilising Criminal Justice: An International Restorative Agenda for Penal Reform* (Waterside Press, U.K., 2013). Among other suggestions, Judge McElrea calls for community justice centers where community members could take their cases directly instead of going through the formal justice process.

[6] Howard Zehr, *Changing Lenses: A New Focus for Crime and Justice* (Herald Press, 1990, 1995, 2005).

[7] James Gilligan, *Violence: Reflections on a National Epidemic* (Random House, 1996).

[8] Daniel Goleman, *Social Intelligence: The New Science of Human Relationships* (Bantam, 2007).

Appendix I

[1] Howard Zehr and Harry Mika, "Fundamental Principles of Restorative Justice," *The Contemporary Justice Review,* Vol. 1, No. 1 (1998), 47-55.

Appendix IV

[1] See http://emu.edu/now/restorative-justice/2009/11/27/10-ways-to-live-restoratively/.

Additional Reading

Little Books of Justice & Peacebuilding
related to restorative justice

David R. Karp, *The Little Book of Restorative Justice for Colleges and Universities.*

Allan MacRae and Howard Zehr, *The Little Book of Family Group Conferences, New Zealand Style.*

Kay Pranis, *The Little Book of Circle Processes.*

Lorraine Stutzman Amstutz, *The Little Book of Victim Offender Conferencing.*

Lorraine Stutzman Amstutz and Judy H. Mullet, *The Little Book of Restorative Discipline for Schools.*

Barb Toews, *The Little Book of Restorative Justice for People in Prison.*

Carolyn Yoder, *The Little Book of Trauma Healing.*

Howard Zehr, *El Pequeño Libro De Justicia Restaurativa.*

Related resources by the author

Changing Lenses: A New Focus for Crime and Justice
(Herald Press, 1990, 1995, 2005).

Doing Life: Reflections of Men and Women Serving Life Sentences
(Good Books, 1996, 2010).

Transcending: Reflections of Crime Victims
(Good Books, 2001).

What Will Happen to Me? with Lorraine Stutzman Amstutz
(Good Books, 2011).

Critical Issues in Restorative Justice, with Barb Toews
(Lynne Rienner, 2004).

"Restorative Justice Blog," with Carl Stauffer, available at
http://emu.edu/now/restorative-justice/.

The Zehr Institute for Restorative Justice
(webinar series and other resources) available at
http://emu.edu/cjp/restorative-justice/.

About the Author

Howard Zehr has been called the "grandfather" of restorative justice, beginning his work as a practitioner and theorist in the late 1970s at the foundational stage of the field. He directed the first formal victim offender conferencing program in the U.S. and is one of the original developers of restorative justice as a concept. A prolific writer and editor, speaker, educator, and photojournalist, Zehr actively mentors other leaders in the field.

His book *Changing Lenses: A New Focus for Crime and Justice* is considered a foundational work in restorative justice. His many other publications include *Doing Life: Reflections of Men and Women Serving Life Sentences*; *Transcending: Reflections of Crime Victims*; and *What Will Happen to Me?* He has spoken and trained others throughout North America and in more than 25 other countries.

Zehr is Distinguished Professor of Restorative Justice and co-director of the Zehr Institute for Restorative Justice at The Center for Justice and Peacebuilding, Eastern Mennonite University (Harrisonburg, Virginia). Zehr received his B.A. from Morehouse College, his M.A. from the University of Chicago, and his Ph.D. from Rutgers University.

THE LITTLE BOOK OF
Victim Offender Conferencing

Bringing Victims and Offenders
Together in Dialogue

LORRAINE STUTZMAN AMSTUTZ

Table of Contents

Acknowledgments

A special thanks to all who courageously enter into a dialogue. Although the work often is painful, it's also transformative. I also am grateful to those who passionately and compassionately respond to the needs of victims and offenders. You are an inspiration to me.

Thanks to Jim and our children, Solomon, Jordan, and Leah, who continue to remind me that what really matters is how we practice what we preach with those we love most. You love me far beyond what I sometimes deserve.

Introduction

Several years ago, my three-year-old son came running into the house with a large red welt under his eye. "Kyle kicked me," he sobbed.

As a parent, my first reaction was to head out the back door to find the boy, a six-year-old, who had hurt my son. Instead I got ice for Jordan's eye and held him until he stopped crying. I read him a book and then he got off my lap and went to play with his toys. About 15 minutes later he came back and asked to go outside to play. I told him he could, but he looked at me and said, "I can't. He might hurt me again."

Since we had lived in the neighborhood only a short time, I did not know which was Kyle's house, but I knew the general area. I took Jordan by the hand and told him we were going to talk to Kyle about what had happened. I told Jordan I would be there to keep him safe. The third door I knocked on was opened by a young woman I recognized as Kyle's mother. I explained to her that the boys had been playing together and Jordan, who was obviously injured, had come in crying. I asked if we could talk to Kyle about what had happened.

Kyle appeared at the top of the stairs with a look of fright on his face as he saw us in the doorway. I asked him to tell me what had happened. He explained that they were playing cops and robbers, and that he was chasing Jordan when Jordan fell. He said he tried to grab Jordan and that he kicked him but didn't mean to hurt him. He ran away because he *was scared he would get into trouble. Kyle's mom scolded him for not helping Jordan when he realized that Jordan was hurt. She also asked if he had anything else to say.*

Kyle looked at Jordan and said, "It looks like your eye really hurts. I'm sorry."

There was silence and his mom said, "Is there anything else you want to say?" Again he looked at Jordan and said, "Will you still be my friend?"

Jordan looked at me and then at Kyle and said, "Will you hurt me again?"

"No," Kyle replied.

Jordan said, "Okay."

I continued to talk to Kyle's mom for a few minutes, and then Jordan and I headed back across the driveway. As we got to our house, Jordan looked up at me and said, "Mom, my eye doesn't hurt anymore."

• • •

My son is now grown, but this story demonstrates the power of Victim Offender Conferencing (VOC), not only in situations involving crime but also in everyday life. VOC is a dialogue process for bringing together people who have harmed and have been harmed to hear each other's stories and to explore ways to repair those harms.

About this book

This book provides an overview of VOC, a process being used in many communities to bring victims and offenders of crime into dialogue with one another. VOC is one of a number of approaches or models that fall within the overall framework of restorative justice.[1]

Introduction

This is not a how-to book on practicing VOC but an overview of the processes that have been developed over the past three decades. It focuses primarily on the North American experience, although forms of VOC are used in other parts of the world.

Restorative justice as a field of theory and practice dates back to the early 1970s. However, some indigenous communities have a much longer history of using restorative justice processes for handling crime. Judge Joseph Flies-Away, a member of the Hualapai Nation, sees this approach as a return to the ways of indigenous people that have been lost through colonization. He points out that when a Hualapai person commits a criminal act, people say, "He acts like he has no relatives." Judge Flies-Away writes,

> **"The purpose of law is to bring the person back into the fold, to heal him. People do the worst things when they have no ties to people."**

"The purpose of law is to bring the person back into the fold, to heal him. People do the worst things when they have no ties to people. Tribal court systems are a tool to make people connected again."[2]

In many ways, restorative justice and approaches such as VOC are Western ways of implementing what many indigenous and traditional cultures have been practicing for generations.

The processes in this *Little Book* were developed primarily within the context of the Western legal system to address some of its deficiencies. Specifically, victim offender dialogues were designed to hold offenders accountable to the person they harmed and to give victims a voice and an opportunity to have their needs met. VOC acknowledges that crime creates a relationship and a connection between the victim and offender. The basic approach of VOC holds possibilities beyond the legal system, and is proving useful to other settings that address wrongdoing, such as schools.

This book, then, provides an introduction to VOC and is useful for those interested in developing a VOC program, facilitating dialogues, or participating in an encounter process that this book describes.

1.
What Is VOC?

I had a switchblade and my accomplice had a sharp kitchen knife that we used to slash 24 car tires. We slashed car seats and destroyed a car radiator. We threw rocks through large plate glass windows in homes and the front window at the local beer store. We pulled a boat into the tree and punctured and overturned it. We damaged a gazebo, a flashing light at an intersection, and broke a cross from a display case at a local church. We used beer bottles to smash car windows and windshields, threw a table into a fishpond, and destroyed a fence. In all, 22 properties were damaged in about a two-hour span. When we finally had enough of this craziness, we headed back to the apartment and passed out.[3]

• • •

These are the words of Russ Kelly, one of the two offenders in the so-called "Elmira Case" in Ontario, Canada, in 1974. Although restorative justice has many roots, the field as a whole is often traced to this initial case.

Mark Yantzi, a probation officer and a volunteer with Mennonite Central Committee (MCC), and a second MCC worker, Dave Worth, were frustrated by the ways offenders were cycling through the system without taking responsibility for what they had done to their victims and the community. They suggested to the judge that the two offenders in this case go back and meet the people they had harmed. After some hesitation, the judge sentenced the offenders to do this. Kelly continues his story:

• • •

Meeting our victims was one of the hardest things I had ever done in my entire life. Accompanied by Mark Yantzi and Dave Worth, we walked up to the victims' front doors to apologize, hear what the victims had to say, determine the amount of restitution, ask for forgiveness, and assure the victims that they were not targeted. It was a random act of vandalism.

Some victims offered forgiveness while others wanted to give us a good whipping. Nonetheless, we survived meeting the victims of our crime spree and returned a couple of months later with certified checks to restore the amount of out-of-pocket expenses not covered by insurance.

• • •

Today Russ Kelly is a staff member at Community Justice Initiatives of Waterloo, Ontario, and is a promoter of restorative justice philosophy.

The current Western restorative justice movement began by bringing victims and offenders together in a facilitated process that was originally called "victim offender reconciliation programs" or VORP. While this name is now used less frequently (the issue of terminology is addressed on pages 124-125), the basic approach is still the most common application of restorative justice, at least in North America.

The VOC process brings victims and offenders of crime together in a face-to-face meeting prepared and led by a trained facilitator, often a community volunteer, to talk about the impact and consequences of the crime. Other family members, friends, and community members also may be involved. This meeting is conducted in a safe and structured setting and gives victims a chance to tell their story, express their feelings, seek answers to questions that the legal process has been unable to

> **The conference holds offenders accountable to the persons they harmed.**

provide and, in most cases, discuss restitution options.

Offenders are also given an opportunity to talk about what happened, to take responsibility for their actions, and to hear personally how their actions impacted the victim. The conference holds offenders accountable to the persons they harmed and makes them part of developing a plan to make restitution.

In the United States, VORP was first implemented in Elkhart, Indiana, in the mid-1970s. The program was based in part on a model formed in Kitchener, Ontario, and initially was operated out of the probation department. It was soon turned over to a nonprofit community organization, Elkhart County PACT (Prisoners and Community Together), and continues under the community-based Center for Community Justice. Many programs developed over the next three decades were based on the Kitchener and Elkhart models.

The Elkhart model worked, almost from the outset, with both juvenile and adult offenders. Many other early programs focused primarily on the juvenile justice system. The intent for many of those programs was to begin in the juvenile system, establish credibility, and then begin taking adult cases as well. In the Elkhart program, practitioners found similarities between adults and juveniles in terms of victim responses and offender accountability.

The early referrals for programs were mostly property crimes such as theft, but "personal" crimes such as simple assault, burglaries, and robberies began to be referred as well. Some programs began working with crimes of severe violence but only after receiving advanced training and procedures (see Chapter 4).

In 1994, the American Bar Association endorsed VOC for use in U.S. courts. By 2000, more than 1,000 victim offender programs were operating in North America and Europe.[4] These programs are administered by private community-based agencies, probation departments, and victim service agencies. Many programs utilize trained community volunteers as case facilitators.

Terminology

In the late 1970s when the first VORP program was initiated in the United States, there was much discussion about appropriate terminology for the process. The term "mediation" was initially discarded because it brought to mind parties who were on somewhat equal moral ground. This is not the case with victims and offenders, in which one party clearly has wronged another.

The primary focus of VORP was to assist victims and offenders in dealing with the relational aspects of crime. Thus the term "reconciliation" was initially used as a way to talk about how face-to-face meetings could work at that relational aspect. The meetings were not intended to provide a "Kumbayah" moment, where people would hug and everything would be all right. Rather, the meetings were seen as a way to acknowledge the harm and injury to individual and community relationships caused by crime.

There was no attempt to force reconciliation between parties. Still, the term "reconciliation" raised legitimate concerns, and many programs opted to use the term Victim Offender Mediation (VOM) rather than VORP.

More recently, some programs have begun dropping "mediation" and "reconciliation" in favor of "conferencing" or "dialogue." Mediation is often viewed as a process that requires participants to adapt to it rather than a flexible process that adapts to the participants. "Mediation" also suggests to victims that they will be negotiating away their right to restitution.

The term "conferencing" suggests a participatory approach that gives flexibility concerning who is included, even making room for community members if appropriate. It was introduced by the Family Group Conferences that became central to New Zealand's youth justice system in 1989.

The following case summary provides one example of why victims and offenders might choose to participate in a face-to-face dialogue.

• • •

A pair of new sneakers had been stolen from the boys' locker room at school. The offender's mother turned him in to the principal and the shoes were returned. The two teenagers did not know each other but both agreed to mediation. When asked what restitution he wanted, the victim said he only needed to hear the other kid's apology and hoped it would help him learn a lesson.

Would there really be any satisfaction, particularly for the victim? There was palpable tension at the beginning of the joint meeting. While this did not go away totally, things relaxed somewhat when the offender apologized to the victim. Later the victim's mother expressed her appreciation to the offender's mother for turning her son in to the principal. And when the victim said he accepted the apology, hoped the offender had learned a lesson, and was not asking for any restitution, it seemed to surprise the offender.

I do not anticipate that these two parties will become friends, but the mediation will allow them to move on without the burden of guilt, anger, and nagging questions. That makes it worth the effort.[5]

• • •

The VOC process

The process in a typical VOC follows the same basic steps, regardless of whether the case involves single or multiple victims and offenders. The steps include:

1. **Referral**
   Cases are referred by various sources, including judges, probation or police officers, prosecutors, or community agencies. Criteria and protocols for this are usually worked out with the referral source.

2. **Screening and case management**
   The referral is logged into a case management system and screened for suitability. A program staff member then assigns the case to a trained facilitator.

3. **First contact**

   The facilitator checks with the offender first to make sure he or she is willing to proceed, then contacts the victim. Initial contact with the victim is by letter, with a follow-up phone call.

4. **Initial meetings**

   Separate face-to-face meetings with the victim and offender provide an opportunity for the facilitator to hear each story, explain the VOC process, determine willingness to proceed, find an appropriate time and place for the conference, and prepare participants for the meeting. The facilitator also helps the victim and offender identify support people they want in attendance, such as a family member, friend, mentor, or pastor.

5. **Support people**

   As in Step 4, support people attend the conference at the request of the victim or offender, and with the agreement of the primary participants. The facilitator meets separately with the support people before the conference to explain the process and their role. If a meeting is not possible, this conversation happens via phone.

6. **The conference**

   After basic ground rules or guidelines are clarified, the conference provides an opportunity for the primary participants and support people to talk about their experiences and feelings and to ask questions of each other. Participants then explore what is needed to address the harms and losses sustained by the victim, recognizing that no restitution agreement can fully replace the losses, but is largely symbolic. Finally, the parties sign the restitution agreement and, if they previously knew each other, a behavioral agreement that guides their future interaction.

7. **Reporting and monitoring**
   The facilitator reports on the meeting to the program staff. A copy of the agreement and a brief report is sent to the referring agency. The program then monitors the agreement until it has been completed, and helps to work out any snags.

8. **Closing the case**
   Once restitution is completed, some programs provide an opportunity for the parties to meet to celebrate the agreement's completion. A final report is sent to the referring agency.

Other dialogue processes

VOC is just one restorative justice process. The following illustrates the range of approaches for when victims and offenders come together in dialogue.

VOC processes were initially conceived as bringing together one victim and one offender, but from early on the process included as many people as necessary. Many communities continue to adapt and blend these processes.

Family Group Conferencing

The Family Group Conferencing (FGC) models from New Zealand (and later adopted in Australia) have played a significant role in bringing a broader representation of family, friends, community members, and sometimes justice personnel into the process. The New Zealand model emphasizes family empowerment, cultural suitability, consensus decision making, and use of a family caucus during the conference.

FGC originated in New Zealand as a way to relieve an overburdened juvenile justice system crowded with indigenous Maori youth. The FGC approach incorporated Maori values that emphasize the role of family and community in a justice process.[6] FGC was enacted into New Zealand law in 1989 and became the standard for processing juvenile cases, with the exception of cases involving murder/manslaughter. Since implementing FGC, juvenile judges have reported 80 percent fewer cases.[7]

Family Group Decision Making (FGDM)

During the mid-1990s, FGDM was adapted from the New Zealand FGC model and became widely used within the child welfare system in the United States. The National Center on Family Group Decision Making, a program of the American Humane Society, describes the values of FGDM:

> [FGDM is] rooted in the belief that families have a shared history, wisdom, untapped resources, and an unrivaled commitment to their children. It is about empowering families and their friends to think and plan creatively for their children, create community partnerships, and utilize family strengths to resolve child welfare concerns. It is also an invitation to families to be responsible for the outcomes of a plan of their own creation.[8]

The FGDM process is typically coordinated through child welfare agencies, which solicit voluntary participation by families where there is a substantiated case of abuse or neglect. As in victim offender and family/community conferencing cases, preparation meetings are a key component.

Preparation includes ensuring the child's safety, as well as identifying extended family members and support people who are invited into the process. Involving those who have caused the harm is also critical, because they need to be involved in determining and implementing solutions.

Just as in victim offender and family/community conferencing, follow-up is critical. Child safety often depends on the coordinating agency closely monitoring the delivery of services and communicating decisions made at the meeting. There are times when follow-up meetings are held to review the case or to renegotiate agreements.

Circle Processes

Circle Processes draw directly from the tradition of the Talking Circle, common among indigenous people of North America. Kay Pranis writes in *The Little Book of Circles Processes*:

> Gathering in a Circle to discuss important community issues was likely a part of the tribal roots of most people. Such processes still exist among indigenous people around the world, and we are deeply indebted to those who have kept these practices alive as a source of wisdom and inspiration for modern Western cultures.[9]

Circle Processes often expand the number of people involved in the dialogue. These participants identify the values they want to guide the process. Usually these dialogues employ a talking piece, an item that holds symbolic meaning to the group and which is passed from person to person, giving that person the right to speak. Facilitators are often called the "Circle Keeper" and require a different form of training than facilitators of VOC.

> **As Circles become more widely used in Western culture, it's critical to adapt them in culturally appropriate ways.**

Circles assume various names that reflect their uses, including Peacemaking Circles, Healing Circles, Talking Circles, Care Circles, and School Circles. Because Circles resonate with so many traditions and because they are so inclusive and powerful, they have wide cultural appeal for many participants.

Circle Processes include these tenets:

- Each person wants to be connected to others in a good way.

- Each is a valued member of the community and has a right to his or her beliefs.

- We all share some core values that indicate what connecting in a good way means, even though being connected in a good way and acting from our values are not always easy, especially amid difficulty or conflict.[10]

As Circles become more widely used in Western culture, it's critical to adapt them in culturally appropriate ways rather than simply importing the symbols or approaches of other cultures. Val Napoleon, of Cree-Saulteaux-Dunne Zah heritage, warns against "romanticizing human beings, cultures, or communities, because this will short-circuit the necessary critical and creative thought required to create positive social change through restorative justice."[11]

Values underlying the processes

Much work has been done to identify the framework and processes of restorative justice. The Office on Justice & Peacebuilding at Mennonite Central Committee, where I work, uses the following value statements to guide its work:

- All people should be treated with dignity and respect, recognizing that each person has some piece of the truth.

- Each of us needs to be responsible for our own actions and needs to be held accountable for those actions.

- By our presence we are all members of communities and therefore connected to one another.

- We recognize that forgiveness is a process that allows all people to walk at their own pace.

- We provide opportunities for reconciliation as appropriate and as defined by those affected by the actions of others.

Because of its emphasis on individuality, Western society is sometimes called a "low context" environment. In a "high context" environment, the dominating world-view focuses on oneness with others and the importance of community.

These values are evident in a culture's legal system. Within a Western legal system, rooted in individualism, each person is responsible for his or her actions against another, and the system speaks for the victims. This emphasis on the individual versus the community contributes to the mistrust that many non-Western people feel toward the Western legal system.

The values that guide VOC processes are best understood within the context of a web. Any process or framework must be connected to larger social and justice issues rather than an individualistic response to crime. These values include the following:

- **Interconnectedness**
  Processes should include all those affected and should address the social, systemic, spiritual, and personal implications.

- **Respect**
  All human beings have inherent and equal value, regardless of their actions, race, class, gender, age, beliefs, sexual orientation, or status in society. Respect includes listening, speaking, and mutual consideration and understanding of participants.

- **Transparency**
  A complete and honest understanding of motivation is essential, to the extent possible.

- **Accountability**
  All participants have an obligation to engage and participate in the process, to accept responsibility for their actions and the impact of those actions on others, and to amend their actions as needed.

- **Self Determination**
  A process should encourage empowerment of all participants.

- **Spirituality**
  A process has the capacity to reach beyond the people involved. A process should inspire healing and change in the participants, and faith in a strengthened community. While the processes described here are not explicitly religious or spiritual, many participants perceive a spiritual quality in the process.

- **Truth**
  It is important that people speak their truth, which is more than the discovery of facts. This truth-telling happens as people tell their stories about their experiences in a safe and caring environment.

As this chapter demonstrates, VOC continues to evolve in scope and terminology, and is one dialogue process among several that has emerged from the restorative justice framework.

2.
Motives for Participating in a VOC Process

*I*t was mid-week, a slow night for the local convenience store. Fifteen-year-old Scott entered the store with two friends, who appeared to be armed, and demanded the money in the cash drawer. The owners remained calm and handed over about $100 in cash. The boys left and divided up the cash.

When we met Scott, he was in the process of trying to turn around his life. He had completed his high school equivalency degree, found a job, had an apartment, and now, at 17, was willing to face his victim and be held accountable for his crime. We also met with the store owners, Ruth and Nathan. Ruth was still upset about what had happened but agreed to meet with Scott.

In the joint meeting, Ruth asked Scott to speak first. It was important for her to have some questions answered: Why did they pick her store? Was his crime worth the small amount of cash? Did he realize the crime's impact on her? What was he doing with his life now?

She seemed relieved to learn that the store had been picked at random and that the crime definitely wasn't worth it. Scott had committed the robbery because he was broke, living on his own (having been kicked out of his house), and couldn't find work. It was a low point in his life, and *he was desperate. He admitted that while he would never truly know what Ruth had been through, he could imagine some of her trauma.*

The discussion flowed naturally. Ruth had not known at the time that the weapons were only pellet guns and had felt paralyzed with fear at the thought of leaving her children as orphans. She no longer thought of her community as a safe place and needed to know that Scott was no longer committing crimes. Scott apologized and assured Ruth he would commit no more crimes.

Ruth expressed concern that Scott would lose his job if he had to go to jail. She offered to attend Scott's court hearing, even though she was not required to do so. Her testimony influenced the judge to suspend enough of the jail sentence that Scott wouldn't lose his job.

Both parties came to the initial conference with apprehension. Scott was terrified about meeting his victim face-to-face. Ruth was afraid of how angry she would be and of what memories she might re-live at meeting her offender. Neither expected the personal connection they made.[12]

• • •

The experience of victimization is often devastating and affects people in profound, life-altering ways. Whether the crime is "minor" or "serious," the effects can be traumatic. Victims experience a range of emotions that include intense fear, helplessness, and anger at themselves and others, including family, friends, and the legal system. Some victims may experience a crisis of faith as they reassess their belief in a protective God. Many ask whether the harm was their own fault and struggle with a loss of control over their own lives, which leads to isolation from others.

These responses to crime create needs that can be met in a variety of ways. Sometimes victims' immediate and broader communities can provide a sense of safety and justice. But some needs can be met only by the person who caused the harm.

Researchers at the Center for Restorative Justice and Peacemaking at the University of Minnesota reviewed 85 studies to examine participants' motives for entering into restorative justice dialogues. The studies included participants of victim offender mediation, group conferencing, Circles, and other community-based processes.[13]

Various motives for victim participation included a desire to receive restitution (whether financial or otherwise), wanting to hold the offender accountable, and learning more about the "why" of the crime. Victims also expressed a need to share their pain with offenders as well as receive assurances that they would not commit a repeat offense. Perhaps most importantly, victims needed to believe they were involved in an experience that helped them to regain power and respect following their victimization. Significantly, the report found that while restitution was the primary motivator for participating in victim offender mediation, what victims most valued was the opportunity to talk with the offender.[14]

Some victim needs can only be met by the person who caused the harm.

In the same study, offenders gave numerous reasons for participating in a dialogue with their victims. Many believed the dialogue process would help them put the crime behind them and move on. They cited being able to have a say in determining and paying restitution, being able to talk about what happened to the victim, and being able to apologize for what they did as important facets of the dialogue.

The following story from a victim offender program in Ohio illustrates some of these motivations at work.

• • •

One evening, 14-year-old John was throwing rocks from a bridge and broke the windshield of a semi-truck passing underneath. He was caught by a passerby who observed the incident. He then was arrested.

When the facilitator contacted the victim, Mr. Owens, he said he had no interest in meeting with the boy, even though he acknowledged that it was a traumatic event that could have taken his life. A few days later, after thinking it over, Mr. Owens contacted the office and said he had changed his mind and wanted to say a few things to John.

It was an important meeting for both of them. John learned how much the incident had traumatized Mr. Owens and about the losses he experienced. Driving a truck had been the victim's livelihood and his first love, and now he lived daily with a new fear. As part of the restitution agreement, Mr. Owens asked John to come and help him wash his truck each Saturday for a month. The arrangement worked well and Mr. Owens believed that the relationship they developed during those Saturday mornings was very positive.

On the last Saturday, however, John called to say that he couldn't come because his father had been killed in a car accident the night before. Mr. Owens decided to attend John's father's funeral and committed to being a "big brother" to John.[15]

• • •

Crime creates a relationship, albeit a negative one. The brokenness affects not only those directly involved but also family members, friends, and the communities to which the victim and offender belong. The dialogue that takes place within VOC focuses on addressing that brokenness.

This is reflected in victims' statements such as, "It gave us a chance to see each other face to face and to resolve what happened," and "It minimized the fear I would have as a result of being a victim because I got to see that the offender was human, too."[16]

Offenders have said that, "After meeting the victims, I now realize that I hurt them a lot," and, "Through mediation, I was able to understand a lot about what I did. I realized that the victim really got hurt, and that made me feel really bad."[17]

The following story demonstrates the potential that VOC holds for both victims and offenders who come together in dialogue.

• • •

The offender worked in the shoe department of a local retail store. She was caught on video by the security manager stealing cash from the register.

The offender initially did not want to face her victims. She was embarrassed at what she'd done and was afraid of being yelled at and "grilled" again by the security manager. It took time, but after consulting with her mom, she agreed to meet. She also requested that the store supervisor attend the mediation because of the good relationship they had enjoyed and because the supervisor felt like a "safe" person.

During a preparation meeting with the store supervisor and security manager, it was clear the supervisor felt victimized personally because she had worked directly with the offender. The corporation, represented by the security manager, was a victim also, but on a monetary basis rather than personally.

Initially the meeting was difficult because the offender cried a lot and had a hard time talking about her offense. She was anxious but able to express her remorse. She seemed surprised that the security manager was not a "mean person" after all.

The store supervisor talked about how personal the offense was to her and how she now had a hard time trusting any of the other employees. That statement seemed to affect the offender profoundly. The offender's mom also talked about the impact this experience had had on her family.

The participants reached an agreement regarding restitution, which was paid on the spot.[18]

3.
Steps in the VOC Process

We now turn to a more detailed description of the VOC process and the steps involved. The diagram below shows the steps in a typical VOC process, from case referral to the final, follow-up meeting.

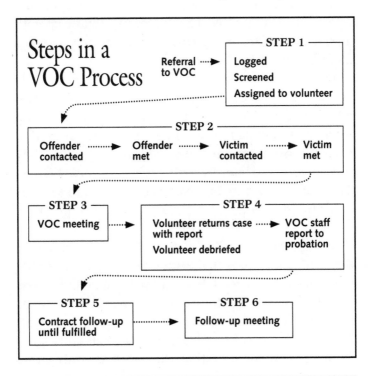

Steps in a VOC Process

Referral to VOC ····▶

STEP 1
Logged
Screened
Assigned to volunteer

STEP 2
Offender contacted ········▶ Offender met ········▶ Victim contacted ········▶ Victim met

STEP 3
VOC meeting ·····▶

STEP 4
Volunteer returns case with report ·····▶ VOC staff report to probation
Volunteer debriefed

STEP 5
Contract follow-up until fulfilled ·············▶

STEP 6
Follow-up meeting

Referral to VOC

Programs receive cases from a predetermined referral source, which can include probation services, police officers, youth aid panels, prosecutors, judges, schools, or community groups. Some programs work with only one or two referral sources; others receive referrals from many different points in the justice process. Written protocols and understandings with such sources prescribe the referral processes.

Step 1 – Logging, screening, and assignment

When a referral is made to a VOC program, it is logged into the program's case management system. A letter is sent to the offender that introduces the program and informs him or her that a facilitator will follow up with a phone call. Most programs then assign the case to a facilitator or co-facilitators.

The facilitator assigned to the case receives a file containing pertinent information, such as names, addresses, and phone numbers of the victim and offender. Other key information may include whether multiple offenders are involved and whether they will be referred later by a different probation officer. The status of others involved is of interest to victims and offenders when a facilitator calls to schedule a meeting.

Most programs wait to contact the victim until after the initial meeting with the offender to assess his or her willingness to proceed. In the past, if the offender was unwilling to meet with the victim, the program never contacted the victim. More recently, however, programs have begun contacting victims to ask about other ways to meet their needs rather than just assuming that the program cannot provide any other services if an offender doesn't want to meet.

Even though the referral source has decided that the case is appropriate for a VOC, program staff also screen cases at this point. The screening ensures that the offender takes some level of responsibility and that there are no serious behavioral or safety concerns regarding the victim or the offender. If such concerns exist, the case may be rejected or accepted with certain precautions. Facilitators are trained to be alert for such screening issues in subsequent phases of the process.

Step 2 – Initial meetings

The facilitator's first phone call involves scheduling an introductory meeting with the offender to explain the process and listen to the offender's story. If the offender (and parent or guardian, if the offender is a juvenile) agrees to meet with the victim, this process is repeated with the victim.

During these initial meetings, participants are asked about others they would like to have present during the joint conference. The facilitator then schedules meetings with these other supporters. These face-to-face meetings are extremely important and help to establish trust, address concerns about safety or procedure, and anticipate possible dynamics of the meeting.

Once all participants have agreed to meet, the conference is scheduled. The facilitator takes care to ensure that the meeting place is agreeable to all participants and that the environment provides a safe space for all involved.

Step 3 – The VOC meeting

The conference is the time to explore what happened. Participants, including support people, are encouraged to talk about their experiences and feelings as well as to ask questions of each other.

The conference also explores what is needed to address the harms and losses, recognizing that much of what offenders agree to is merely symbolic of the losses that occurred. The facilitator makes sure that any agreements are realistic and specific enough for the program staff to monitor. Participants also discuss whether a future meeting is needed after the agreement is met to acknowledge and validate the process.

Step 4 – Reporting and debriefing

After the conference, the facilitator reports back to the VOC staff and returns the signed restitution agreement and participant evaluation form (if any were completed). The facilitator then debriefs with program staff.

Step 5 – Contract follow-up

VOC staff return the agreement form to the referral source and begin monitoring the restitution agreement. This involves ensuring that the offender follows through on the agreement and that the victim is kept informed of the status, particularly if a problem with completion occurs.

Step 6 – Follow-up meeting

Once the offender fulfills the agreement, the facilitator arranges a final meeting if the participants request one. This final meeting is one ritual that allows participants to meet informally to acknowledge the fulfilled agreement and bring a sense of closure to the process. Many victims and offenders find it helpful to hear the other's appreciation for the process.

If a final meeting is not desired, the VOC staff notify the referral source that the offender has completed restitution. The referral source then follows through on next steps, which often include a release from probation, assuming other tasks have been completed.

Sometimes the outcome of the VOC can impact the overall outcome of the case. If the case is referred as a diversion from prosecution, for example, a successful VOC agreement may be accepted in lieu of prosecution. If the case is referred by the court, after adjudication but before sentencing, the judge may take the restitution agreement into account when sentencing.

While the overall process of all VOC programs is similar, the specifics depend in part on a program's design and institutional base. Where referrals come from; who initiates contact with victims and offenders (and in which order); whether referrals are accepted for juveniles, adults, or both; and at what stage in the legal process referrals are made are all variables that differ from program to program.

4.
Issues in Designing a VOC Program

In 1998, Howard Zehr and I developed a one-day training for people in Pennsylvania interested in starting a victim offender program. We developed a set of key questions for people to consider before implementing their programs.[19] Those issues and questions, with a few updates, provide an idea of the various forms that VOC programs take.

What is the impetus for the program?

Clarity about goals and reasons for implementing a program help determine the direction a program takes. What are the program's goals? Who is making the decisions about implementation? Are all key community stakeholders involved in planning at the earliest possible stage? These stakeholders include community representatives, such as members of neighborhood faith-based groups, victim advocate groups, and law enforcement, probation, and other legal system representatives.

What will be the criteria for accepting or rejecting cases?

Most VOC programs screen on a case-by-case basis rather than establishing strict criteria. The exception in most programs is domestic violence cases, because an ongoing cycle of violence is present. Once safety for the victim has been established, some programs offer dialogue specific to domestic violence issues, such as child custody, visitation, and finances. But consultation with domestic violence service providers is essential before accepting such cases.

Where in the system will the cases come from?

Referrals to VOC come from many points in the system, although most of the time they are made after the offender has entered the legal system. For adults, the referral usually comes after guilt has been established (often after a guilty plea) and prior to or after sentencing.

With juveniles, the referral process is much more discretionary. Some referrals come immediately upon intake, possibly in conjunction with informal probation or diversion, which eliminates going through a formal court process. Others come after adjudication; that is, after a hearing has taken place and the offender is placed on probation. VOC may be recommended by the judge or probation officer, or it may be ordered by the court as part of a sentence.

Typically, programs receive cases from the legal system once someone has entered the criminal justice system. This is a source of criticism, particularly from victim advocates, that VOC is an offender-driven process. Referrals also may come from other community institutions such as churches and schools.

Are all offenders who participate required to admit guilt?

In most cases, the VOC process follows an offender's admission of involvement. Occasionally, an offender may admit to something different than what the formal charges state, which can lead to a useful discussion among participants during the conference.

Some VOC programs require the offender not only to admit guilt but also to express remorse and be ready to offer an apology. However, it is often during the meeting with the victim, and hearing his or her story, that the offender feels and experiences remorse. In this light, VOC is best understood as an *opportunity* for the offender to be held accountable to the person harmed and to take responsibility for that harm, whether or not the offender shows remorse or apologizes. It is important that the facilitator not set up expectations in initial meetings with the victim regarding an apology from the offender.

Does VOC work for both juvenile and adult cases?

Yes, although programs often start by working with juveniles. Some believe this process makes a greater impact on juveniles and may deter them from becoming repeat offenders. For some programs, the referral source determines what kinds of cases to refer, and many find the juvenile legal system more amenable to VOC programs than the adult system.

However, after VOC programs develop confidence and expertise, they often move into the adult system as well. Given that holding someone accountable is one goal of any restorative justice process, it follows that VOC can be successful with adults and juveniles.

Is this a voluntary process on the part of the victim and offender?

In some programs, the decision to enter into a dialogue process is, in fact, victim-initiated. Where this is not the case, victims should never feel coerced into any process. It is common for victims to be reluctant to enter into a dialogue process. Therefore, careful preparation is key in order to hear a victim's concerns and help them decide whether to proceed.

Programs vary in regard to offender participation. There may be an element of coercion for offenders, although it is clear that coercing anyone into a process likely will lead to an unsuccessful outcome. Yet offenders generally are not eager to meet face to face with the person they have harmed. Many have said it is easier to go to jail than to meet their victims.

Rather than frame the process in terms of being "voluntary" or "mandatory," it is helpful to encourage this as a means for achieving accountability and taking responsibility for the harm caused. If offenders believe that accountability is important in helping them move forward, they often are much more likely to participate.

Who should be involved in the victim offender process?

In the early days of victim offender programs, the victim and offender were the primary participants. While others were occasionally invited to sit in, the conferences were limited to those directly involved. In juvenile cases, the parents sometimes were included if they chose.

This understanding has evolved significantly over the years. VOC programs learned from the Family Group Conferences (FGC) model that the process is intended to empower all participants to acknowledge harm, not only to the primary victim but also to secondary victims such as family and community members. The following story illustrates the power of family and community in an FGC process.

• • •

Six 15-year-old boys walking through a school parking lot after baseball practice decided to use their bats to hit balls through the windows of a parked pick-up truck. The owner of the truck, a retired electrician who drove a bus for some of the sports teams to their games, was devastated when he saw the damage. He reported the incident to the school administration, who over the next three weeks tried to determine who had damaged Mr. Jacks's vehicle.

Mr. Jacks finally learned the names of the six boys who were responsible. After initial denials, the boys finally admitted their actions and were told that the criminal offense required police involvement.

This case was referred to the local victim offender program, and facilitators met with Mr. Jacks. He was extremely reluctant to meet with the boys because he believed his truck was targeted for actions he may have taken while driving the sports bus. He acknowledged, however, that he did not know the six boys personally and had no reason to think they had targeted his truck. But he could not imagine any other reason for the destruction of property. He ultimately agreed to meet with the young men if his son could participate in the meeting as a support person.

Meanwhile, meetings were held with the six boys and their parents, including two step-parents who blamed the custodial parents for their sons' acting out. The boys were obviously embarrassed by their actions and acknowledged that this had been a stupid thing to do. They agreed to meet with Mr. Jacks so they could reassure him this wasn't a personal assault and so they could pay him back for the damage they had caused.

They also agreed that the assistant principal, the student council adviser (one boy was student council president), and the baseball coach should be present so that they could see the boys were accepting responsibility after initially denying their involvement. Mr. Jacks agreed to these participants' attendance in the meeting, along with his son.

The two-hour meeting allowed all participants to talk about what happened. It was important for Mr. Jacks and his son to learn that this was, in fact, a random act and that the boys did not know it was his pick-up. Mr. Jacks was especially interested in hearing from others in the meeting about consequences the boys had faced at home and in school. He acknowledged the importance of the boys having support during a time when they were engaging in "young and stupid" behavior that obviously could lead to even more serious trouble for them in the future.

While not minimizing the poor choices made by his son, one father agreed that he and his ex-wife, who also attended the meeting, needed to be more respectful of one another rather than continuing to blame the other for choices their son was making. They agreed that family counseling (which would include step-parents) would be a helpful next step.

School officials acknowledged how important it was for them to participate. They had been disappointed that the boys had not "come clean" about their involvement until witnesses to the event came forward. Seeing them take responsibility and agree to certain consequences, which involved speaking to their classmates and teammates at school about what happened, gave them hope that this would not happen again. The process enabled school officials to welcome the boys back to the school community and to the baseball team.

• • •

What will be the organizational base?

In the early 1980s, most new programs were community-based nonprofits, often strongly supported by faith communities. While many programs continue with that model, some are operating from other bases, such as the legal system. One of the reasons for using a criminal justice system base (e.g. probation) may be economic. Also, starting a program within the probation department provides more confidence from the courts and avoids issues of credibility that community-based programs need to establish.

A program operated out of the probation department may not be seen as impartial by the victim community.

On the other hand, there are cautions to consider when lodging a program in the legal system. The legal system may have different goals than those established by the program. It may be more focused on offenders than on victims, and on establishing and collecting restitution. While the latter is certainly an important need for victims, it often supersedes the emphasis on understanding other needs that victims may bring to the process.

Another caution to consider is that a program operated out of the probation department will not be seen as impartial by the victim community. Since referrals to most programs come from the legal system, victims often have felt that victim offender programs are simply agents of the legal system, even when they are housed within the community. A program's base within the legal system reinforces that perception.

The advantages of community-based programs include the freedom to set their own criteria for cases; to refuse cases; and to treat certain information as confidential, which may be more difficult when aligned with the legal system. It's more likely that the community as a whole will be better represented than in a program based within the legal system.

The funding may seem more stable in a program housed within the legal system, thus eliminating the need for ongoing fundraising and other administrative issues. However, the reality is that these programs are often secondary to the overall system and are vulnerable to budget elimination.

Who will provide oversight?

It is critical that a group of people representing stakeholders within the community not only provide an organizational base for initial efforts but also ongoing support for program development. One criticism from victim advocates is that they are invited into the conversation once the program has been implemented, but are not included in the initial start-up stage.

If a program is to serve all within a community, then the initial start-up group must include representatives from different groups, such as victim services, rape and domestic violence center directors, probation office chiefs, judges, defense attorneys, district attorneys, and law enforcement. This group will be instrumental in making decisions regarding the program's organizational base and ongoing strategic planning and implementation.

Who will facilitate dialogues?

Most programs use trained community volunteers, although some programs use only trained staff to facilitate dialogues. There are many advantages in utilizing trained community volunteers. While it may be easier to use trained staff—allowing greater flexibility in scheduling meetings and conferences with participants—using volunteers reinforces the need for community involvement in issues of crime.

Community volunteers are seen as primarily concerned with strengthening the community bonds.

Having community members volunteer as facilitators also allows both victims and offenders to feel supported by their community. Community volunteers have a stake in the outcome of the process that differs from those within the system. Those within the system may be regarded suspiciously by the victim and/or the offender, but community volunteers are seen as primarily concerned with strengthening the community bonds.

This is not to diminish the importance of those who work within the system, since many chose this work precisely because they believe in the benefits of VOC programs. It is important, however, to be aware of perceptions toward trained facilitators and to address that issue at the program implementation level.

How will facilitators be trained and supervised?

There is ongoing dialogue in the field around what should be included in the training, how long the training should be, and which training model is best.

While there is no standardized training for certification within the victim offender field, the international Victim Offender Mediation Association (VOMA) has, for a number of years, provided a 24-hour basic victim offender mediation training at its annual conference. This training includes an introduction to a restorative justice framework and philosophy, victim and offender awareness and sensitivity issues, risks and benefits of victim offender mediation, communication skills, conflict resolution skills, the role of the mediator, and an introduction to the dialogue process between victims and offenders. VOMA also maintains a database of trainers who are available to conduct sessions.

VOC programs provide an average of nine to 40 hours of volunteer training. Often the length of training is determined by the program facilitators' experience level, whether a program offers ongoing in-service training, and time or funding constraints. Some states have certification requirements for mediators, which may dictate the number of training hours needed.

Given that fundraising and staffing are ongoing challenges for most victim offender and community mediation programs, many of these organizations are joining together and utilizing the same volunteers. While there are similarities between the programs, differences must be acknowledged. Some differences are evident in the language used. For example, in community mediation, participants are referred to as "disputants." In VOC cases, referring to the offense as a "dispute" would be inappropriate and offensive to the victim.

What is the role of the facilitator?

The facilitator plays a crucial role in the VOC process. In addition to being alert to screening issues, a facilitator must build trust with participants and create a safe space for them, guide the overall process, and ensure that agreements are realistic and appropriate.

The facilitator is not a judge or arbiter who imposes an agreement but rather works to create a space where participants can come to consensus. The facilitator must not take sides or show bias. The mediation field sometimes speaks of facilitators as "neutrals." However, many VOC cases involve someone who has clearly harmed another, and no one can or should be neutral about that. Dave Gustafson, who has pioneered the work of severe violence dialogue, says such facilitation calls not for neutrality but for "balanced partiality."

VOMA has developed a list of Recommended Ethical Guidelines to assist facilitators in meeting the needs of all participants. [20] One principle of the guidelines is to provide "an appropriate structure (e.g. neutral third-party facilitation, procedural guidelines, ground rules, and intentional seating plan) that can neutralize status and power and provide an environment conducive to meaningful dialogue, even in emotionally intense contexts."[21]

> **The facilitator works to create a space where participants can come to consensus.**

These guidelines may not necessarily be relevant in certain cultural contexts. But they are helpful in facilitating processes between victims and offenders and provide important ways of being as a facilitator when preparing and entering into any victim offender process. The values in Chapter 1 are foundational to the role of facilitator.

What are the advantages and disadvantages of co-facilitation?

Co-facilitation provides the advantage of another set of often-needed eyes and ears. Particularly when a conference involves a large number of participants, it is helpful to have one facilitator lead the process and another to watch participants' reactions. Co-facilitators work together to plan the meeting process and also to debrief together and provide feedback to one another after the conference. Co-facilitation is often used so that less experienced facilitators can observe someone with more experience before leading on their own. Co-facilitation is especially helpful to balance demographics of gender, age, ethnicity, or other dynamics related to the case.

There are, however, disadvantages to co-facilitation. Scheduling meetings can be cumbersome as the number of participants grows. Sometimes co-facilitator relationships suffer from a lack of rapport. Hopefully that also becomes a "teachable moment" as facilitators debrief about the experience. Another disadvantage of co-facilitation is simply the shortage of volunteers, which forces some programs to use the sole mediation model.

Cases involving crimes of severe violence almost always use co-facilitators because of the nature and severity of the harm caused. Cases involving severe violence is discussed further in Chapter 5.

Who contacts victims and offenders?

In the early years of VOC, the facilitators made all of the contacts with victims and offenders. The belief was that these initial contacts began building a level of trust critical to the process. Many programs continue to have facilitators make the initial phone calls to the victims and offenders, but only after sending them a program brochure and a letter informing them that a facilitator will be contacting them.

The initial phone calls to victims and offenders are often difficult to make, and some volunteers don't feel prepared to answer many of the questions that arise. For that reason, some programs have a staff person make the initial contact to secure an agreement to meet. The facilitator then follows up to schedule the meetings.

A third approach in some programs is to have a staff person make the initial contact and schedule the meeting, then assign a facilitator who can meet at that time. Some programs with a large volume of cases have staff conduct the initial meetings with the victim and offender, and then bring in the facilitator for the joint meeting. While this approach may present some problems, many in the field find it efficient for handling a large case load, particularly cases involving minor offenses.

How will confidentiality be addressed?

This is a complex issue and requires careful attention to safeguard trust in the process. In general, facilitators are asked to maintain confidentiality except under specific circumstances as mandated by law. For example, a probation officer who also serves as a community mediator for a case other than his or her own is legally bound to report if an offender admits to another crime during a mediation process.

The presumption of confidentiality extends to all participants. Some programs ask participants to sign a pre-mediation agreement that guarantees confidentiality, unless the agreement developed at the meeting allows otherwise. Some states have statutes that protect the confidentiality of the mediation process, which has led some VOC programs to retain the language of mediation.

How will agreements be monitored?

Proper monitoring of agreements is critical. Usually the victim offender program assumes this role rather than the referral source since the agreement comes out of the victim offender process. Also, referral sources rarely have the resources or the will to do this effectively. Unmonitored agreements that lapse undercut the aim of the VOC process. Victims often feel re-victimized and offenders are not held accountable.

Specific instructions in the written agreement address how the agreement will be fulfilled, so that facilitators can easily monitor it. The agreement details when and how payment will be made. VOC staff regularly contact victims and offenders to ensure that agreements are kept. Sometimes participants need to meet again if the terms or timeline need to be renegotiated. Some programs invite participants to come together upon completing the agreement for a short closing ritual to acknowledge this final step.

What happens when there is no victim offender meeting or when agreements are unfulfilled?

Generally when a participant decides not to meet, the case is returned to the referral source with a letter stating that a meeting will not be taking place. Since this is a voluntary process on the part of the victim, it is not necessary to state the reason for not meeting unless that information is critical for future steps. Given that success may come through means other than a face-to-face meeting, it is important to determine other actions a program may take to benefit the victim or offender.

What other needs does either party have that the program can facilitate?

If a meeting has occurred and the agreement is not being fulfilled, it is important to keep the victim informed. The participants may need to meet again to talk about future steps. It is also important to keep the referral source apprised of any changes in the agreement.

Fortunately, experience shows that most conferences reach agreement. Moreover, the proportion of fulfilled restitution agreements is usually significantly higher than for those ordered by the court.

How will monetary payments be made by offenders and disbursed to victims?

This step varies from program to program and can be as creative as participants, referral sources, and programs allow. Monetary payments can go directly to the victim, with proper documentation, and may happen at the joint meeting. Some programs collect the money and disburse it to the victim on an agreed-upon schedule. Often, when probation officials are the referral source, the money goes through the probation collection office for documentation before it's forwarded to the victims. The key is to be clear about the payment process so that all participants know what the procedure will be.

Does all restitution have to be monetary?

It's important to acknowledge that restitution is often symbolic. It can never atone for the sense of violation that a victim feels. That said, victims often find there are ways offenders can give back a piece of what they have taken. Sometimes victims choose to have their offender do work for them or the community. Sometimes behavioral agreements are part of the restitution, if the victim and offender had a relationship prior to the offense. In any case, program staff need to guide the terms of the agreement and specify how they will monitor and supervise the fulfillment process.

What kind of reports will be made and to whom?

Generally the referral source receives a copy of the agreement form that clearly states the offender's acknowledgment of harm and details the specifics of the agreement. Any meeting notes the facilitator may have kept are destroyed to protect confidentiality.

These are some of the issues to consider when starting a VOC program. Although there are broad similarities in the way VOC programs operate, differences emerge depending on how these questions are answered.

5.
VOC and Crimes of Severe Violence

It had been seven months since I had started the meeting preparation process. It was a long road. In the last conversation before meeting him I thought, "Am I going to reach across the table and strangle him, or will I be calm, cool, and collected?" Right before I went to meet him I got nervous. Why was I doing this? Here I was going to sit face-to-face with someone who killed my mother, a mother I never even got to meet.

At first I couldn't look at him because I didn't know how to react. I was beyond nervous. Panicky. Was I stupid to think I could meet him? It was hard to believe that here I was—the survivor—and I had a hard time looking him in the face! I don't know why! Maybe I was scared of my reaction—I knew what I was capable of. But I was ready for change, a good change.

When I did get in the room with him, it wasn't as bad as I thought it would be. When I finally looked at him, I knew that he was a person who had done a brutal thing. But on the other hand, when I finally did look at him, the contact became easier and smoother.

If I had been vengeful, it would have been easier to say to him, "How could you do something like that?" But I wasn't in that state of mind. I was calmer than I expected, and I cried less than I expected. I was expecting someone who didn't give a crap and had no remorse for what he did. I expected him to be "out there" because he had been a child when this happened and it could have been something he totally forgot about and put out of his mind. But, really, he was very understanding and compassionate.

As the conversation went on, we got to know each other and learned about each other's families. I brought pictures so he could see how I lived through pictures of my mother, children, and family. I had hated him practically all of my life, and I came to talk to him to get rid of my desire for revenge. I wanted him to know that he took from me something I never got a chance to experience. He took from me and my family a mother's love. I can't blame him for the choices I made in my life, but he was wrong for making the choices he had. He needed to accept the responsibility and role he took on by killing a woman he knew nothing about.

After I left I felt a load lift off of me. Emptiness was filled, and anger was diminished. I was still upset that the murder had happened, but I got a chance to talk to the person who knew what had happened. If you walk in with revenge in mind, you won't get anywhere because revenge is a blindfold. You have to be willing to hear what this person says—not just what you want to say.

The hardest part of the conversation was him describing the murder – what he did and how he did it. No one had ever told me about it and now I was talking to the person who was there. Only he could tell me the truth, and I believed what he told me. He admitted what he did. I let go when I walked out the door. I went into this thinking I was doing something for me—but I realized I had done something for him, too.[22]

• • •

Shonna Robinson's story illustrates both the power and the complexity of using VOC in cases of severe violence, such as homicide. Clearly, at least for some people, such an encounter with "the other" offers many benefits. However, facilitating such encounters requires special training, preparation, and safeguards for dealing with this level of harm and trauma.

Dialogues between victims and offenders in crimes of severe violence—homicide, attempted homicide, sexual assault, rape, armed robbery, and other serious harms—have been taking place, at least in a formal, programmatic way, since 1993 in the United States. Canada, through the efforts of the Victim Offender Mediation Program of Community Justice Initiatives in Langley, British Columbia, has an even longer history of such efforts. At this writing, at least 21 states as well as a number of Canadian provinces have such programs, and the number is growing.

Facilitating VOC in cases of severe violence requires special training, preparation, and safeguards.

Most of these dialogues take place in a correctional institution because the offenders in these crimes often serve lengthy prison terms, sometimes life sentences. Currently most of the programs require that victims rather than offenders initiate the process. Canada, however, has done a number of institutionally-generated cases.

Many programs that facilitate severe violence dialogues have waiting lists, as victims and/or survivors are increasingly requesting the opportunity to meet with the person who has caused harm to them or to their loved ones. Victims and survivors give a variety of reasons for wanting to participate in such programs. A four-year study of severe violence encounter programs found that the four most common reasons that victims participate are:

- To seek information

- To show the offender the impact of his or her actions

- To have some form of human contact with the person responsible for the crime

- To advance the healing process[23]

Participation in such programs is voluntary on the part of offenders, but many do agree to meet. In the same study, offenders gave the following reasons for doing so:

- To apologize

- To help victims heal

- To contribute to their own rehabilitation and healing

- To change how their victims viewed them[24]

Unique characteristics of VOC in severe violence

Severe violence conferencing or dialogue differs from the usual VOC in the following ways:

1. Case preparation is significantly longer and more intensive.

This careful preparation can take six months to two years and is a critical element in the process. Facilitators meet multiple times with victims and offenders before any decision is made about whether to meet jointly.

The high level of emotional intensity for victims, offenders, supporters, and facilitators in the preparation time and particularly during the face-to-face meeting (if one is held) requires adequate preparation and support for all involved.

By contrast, community-referred cases often require a short turn-around time due to pending legal issues, including restitution or adjudication, sentencing, probation release, or other issues. Usually in these cases, victims want to work at resolution as soon as possible.

2. The process is victim-initiated.

Cases involving crimes of severe violence are primarily victim-initiated, take place years after sentencing has occurred, and therefore have no bearing on the judicial outcome. Often offenders are incarcerated when victims initiate contact and, while appeals may be pending, cases continue to move forward with the victim's full knowledge of any appeals.

3. Advanced training for facilitators is essential.

Training must go beyond the mechanics of the traditional community-based victim offender model and include an understanding of the psychological trauma of crime as well as the experience of offenders/inmates. Training in the traditional VOC model is not a requirement for facilitators of severe violence.

4. Working with prison officials adds a level of complexity.

Since most meetings occur in prison, good relationships with justice system agencies, particularly state correctional facilities, are obviously essential to the success of any program. This is one reason that many severe violence dialogue programs are operated by victim services organizations attached to the justice system.

5. Facilitators are generally trained staff rather than volunteers.

Staff are generally highly trained in offender treatment issues and victim trauma recovery. This is particularly true for therapeutically-oriented programs that provide intensive and sometimes lengthy follow-up for victims and their family members. However, some programs use volunteer facilitators with good results. Still others use institutional or community resources to provide follow-up care.

Program models

Most programs follow one of three models.

1. The *therapeutic model* focuses on healing and utilizes extensively trained facilitators.

The Texas program, for example, uses this approach "to provide victims of violent crime the opportunity to have a structured face-to-face meeting with their offender(s) in a secure, safe environment in order to facilitate a healing, recovery process."[25]

These programs involve extensive preparation for victims and offenders that includes numerous journaling exercises to assist participants in their recovery process. Post-mediation follow-up is extensive and ongoing, with facilitators maintaining contact with some participants for months and years after mediation. When a case is actually closed often remains uncertain. Although the Texas program has trained community volunteers, many cases are completed by staff using a single facilitator as opposed to other programs that use a co-facilitator model.

2. The *narrative or storytelling model* invites each participant to speak about the crime's impact.

The narrative is determined solely by the participants, with little coaching from facilitators. The focus of the face-to-face meeting is to give participants the opportunity to have a dialogue in a safe and respectful environment. These programs take care to create a safe, supportive process for the victim and offender but focus less on the therapeutic dimensions.

3. The *empowerment model* emphasizes the importance of participants' motives for entering into dialogue.

In the Ohio and Pennsylvania VOC programs, for example, the focus is on empowering victims and offenders to identify their needs and a process for meeting those needs. In this program, the goal of dialogue is not to heal wounds or eliminate grief, but to help participants take a step toward healing.[26]

None of these models is more "right" than the other. As more states and provinces implement dialogues in crimes of severe violence, programs can learn from each other. What all models have in common is a commitment to making the process safe and respectful for both victim and offender. All aim to provide benefits to victims and offenders without coercing any participant.

One woman tells her story of meeting with the man who raped her 24 years earlier.

• • •

My hopes were to have a venue to process feelings I had completely buried for 24 years. At the time of the rape, I was grateful to be alive, and I went back to college, moved on with my life, and never dealt with my trauma. Now I found I needed answers to a seemingly endless number of questions. I also wanted to tell my offender that I forgave him.

At one point I asked to see a current picture of my offender because I never knew for sure if I had seen his face that night. When I looked at the picture, I threw it on the coffee table as terror and disgust flew through me. It was the face of "the monster that had lurked in my closet" for 24 years. At that moment I never wanted to see him again. Eventually I peeked at the picture again and detected a glimmer of light deep in his eyes.

The first time my husband and I met him was good. A lot was accomplished even though it was kind of awkward. When we left that day after the three-hour meeting, I felt very happy but also sort of confused. For some reason it seemed that he did not genuinely want to be there. But as he prepared for our meeting, he had given every impression that he did want to do this.

A week later we learned that he had been seriously ill during our meeting and was admitted to the hospital the very next day. I requested a second meeting to complete what I/we had started.

I finished asking all of my questions and hearing every answer. This time I also shared my true feelings of deep pain and struggle that his crime had caused me. I felt an obligation to do that so he would hear from me—his victim—the reality of what such a violation does to a woman. He listened and cried. He heard me and validated my feelings. He understood. We even laughed a couple of times. Our meeting could not have gone any better.

I now feel like a butterfly that has emerged from her cocoon after 24 years of captivity. I require less sleep and have more energy. I laugh and smile more easily; I am a lot less fearful. I have more peace of mind and less false guilt. I no longer second-guess everything I do. The power and control that were taken from me 24 years ago have been returned by the man who stole them. I don't know if anyone else sees the changes, but I do and my husband does.[27]

• • •

Bringing together victims and offenders in crimes of severe violence should not be entered into lightly. The risk of re-victimization for victims and survivors is great, as is the possibility of serious emotional impact on offenders who may be facing the human consequences of their actions for the first time. As researcher and practitioner Mark Umbreit points out, we still have much to learn, but the experience thus far has been promising.

6.
VOC and the Larger Restorative Justice Field

VOC is part of a larger field called restorative justice. The various dialogue encounters described in Chapter 1 are also part of this field, but the field includes other models as well. Restorative justice is an overall philosophy or framework for understanding and addressing wrongdoing. This chapter briefly describes the concept of restorative justice.

There is no agreed-upon definition of restorative justice. In fact, practitioners disagree about whether there should be one. Some contend that providing too narrow a definition limits the possibilities in the field. Others say a definition is imperative to distinguish genuine restorative justice from practices that use the label but whose approach is contrary to restorative justice principles.

There is, however, widespread agreement on the basic assumptions of restorative justice. These include the importance of addressing the needs of those most affected by crime, needs that often are not met in the traditional legal process. Restorative justice advocates believe that the role of those outside the legal system (victims, offenders, and community members) must be expanded in order for participants' needs to be met.

Three central concepts or assumptions provide the foundation for restorative justice philosophy and practice. These assumptions have roots in many cultural and religious traditions. The assumptions include:

1. Crime is a violation of people and of interpersonal relationships.

2. Violations create obligations.

3. The central obligation is to put right the wrongs.[28]

These assumptions lead to three basic principles:

1. *Restorative justice focuses on harms* rather than on laws or rules that were broken. This means that harm to victims and their needs must be central to restorative justice processes.

2. *Wrongs or harms result in obligations.* Accountability processes should help offenders understand and take responsibility for the harm they have caused. And although the primary obligation may be the offender's, the community may have obligations as well.

3. *Restorative justice promotes engagement or participation.* This includes those who have been harmed and those who have harmed, including members of the community.[29]

Deciding which participants to involve in the justice process is an important component of restorative justice. While the legal system is one stakeholder, the victim, offender, and community should also be part of any process. Ideally, justice is not something done to someone but a collaborative effort of all stakeholders.

The following definition might be seen as a starting point for discussion:

> Restorative justice is an approach that involves, to the extent possible, those who have a stake in a specific offense and to collectively identify and address harms, needs, and obligations, in order to heal and put things as right as possible.[30]

Definitions are risky, however. A Canadian First Nations practitioner, Val Napoleon, asks, "Who decides what restorative justice is, and what are the consequences of these definitions?"[31] Does the definition contain hidden, Eurocentric assumptions? Napoleon recommends that practitioners maintain "a dual perspective on restorative justice that includes seeing the personal within the political and the individual within the collective."[32] In other words, it's imperative to remember that not everyone shares North American values of individualism, and that, for some, the needs and harms of the broader community are just as significant as individual needs.

Justice is not something done to someone but a collaborative effort of all stakeholders.

In addition to these principles, it is important to think about restorative justice in terms of values that promote the integrity of relationships and human connections between individuals and within communities. This suggests that larger social issues must be included in any restorative justice process.

VOC is one of the most widely-known applications of restorative justice. Some presume that the various forms of conferencing are the only applications of restorative justice. Indeed, restorative justice concepts and language initially grew out of VOC.

But if restorative justice has overall validity, its implications must extend beyond conferencing to society at large and to everyday life. Both victim and offender advocacy communities have asked how restorative justice can address the needs of victims and offenders apart from VOC. Those voices have challenged practitioners to look at participants' needs beyond providing opportunities for dialogue once an offender has been caught, arrested, and convicted.

Eric Gilman, Restorative Justice Coordinator for the Clark County, Washington, Juvenile Court, has articulated a hopeful approach to the work of victim offender programs. He argues that the primary focus of any program is larger than encouraging victims to participate in a dialogue process. Rather, the focus should be on "the community pro-actively responding to individuals who have been harmed by crime in ways that meaningfully address their felt needs."[33]

Clearly, the scope of restorative justice must extend beyond face-to-face dialogues, while not minimizing the clear benefits this process currently provides. This larger discussion must include a broader definition of "victims" and "offenders," which has been defined by the legal system with very narrow parameters. For example, a broader definition recognizes that offenders often were first victims themselves.

A broadened scope of restorative justice also must address issues of power. Dennis Sullivan and Larry Tifft explore the implications of restorative justice for society and everyday life:

> When we say that meeting the needs of everyone and expanding our collective potential is central to the principles and practices of restorative justice, we immediately come face to face with issues of power, because an ethic of power justifies satisfying the needs and creating the well-being of some at the expense of others. Power reflects an ideology of differential human worth, whereby one person or group regards itself as having greater value than others. Hence, actions taken for reasons of power—even those that might be said to heal, make things right, foster voice or meet emergent needs—perpetuate violence. They defy the spirit of restorative justice, for they support cultures of privilege and institutionalize patterns of inequality. Clearly, as proponents of restorative justice, we are all called upon, therefore, to examine and understand the workings of power in all aspects of our lives.[34]

The field of restorative justice is at a critical crossroad as it broadens the scope of possibilities and continues to recognize the significance of connections among and between individuals in our communities.

7.
Benefits and Risks
of a VOC Process

T his chapter explores more fully some of the benefits and the potential risks for the various stakeholders in a VOC process. The stakeholders include victims, offenders, communities, and the justice system.[35]

Benefits for victims

In a VOC, victims meet their offenders and, in doing so, talk about their feelings regarding the crime. They may also get answers about their crime that they may not have gotten through the legal process. Why was my house burglarized? Did the offender have something against me personally? What if I had been home? Was my house watched for weeks prior to the burglary? Such questions are very important to victims. VOC encounters often relieve frustrations and reduce the level of anxiety victims may have about the possibility of future victimization.

VOCs also give victims the possibility of receiving restitution for wrongs. Although full restitution for all harms or damages may be impossible, victims often find that even partial restitution is symbolically important. When restitution agreements are made, most have high rates of fulfillment.

Victims who participate in setting an amount and payment schedule often gain a sense of empowerment through the process. Also helpful to victims is hearing offenders acknowledge their wrongdoing and express remorse.

Many victims experience changed attitudes about punishment and offenders, increased understanding of offenders and the nature and causes of crime, and a reduced sense of alienation as a result of this process.

Research Summary

A large multi-site study of VOC found that:

- Victims who participated in a face-to-face encounter were more likely to be satisfied with the justice process (79 percent) compared to similar victims who only went through the traditional legal system (57 percent).

- 90 percent of victims were satisfied with the mediation process.

- After meeting the offender, victims' fears of being re-victimized were significantly reduced.

Victims who participated in VOC expressed themes of empowerment, such as feeling involved in the justice process, giving voice to opinions and emotions, and having a sense of emotional healing.[36]

Risks for victims

Victims sometimes feel they would rather simply move on from the crime instead of participating in a process that brings up painful feelings relating to the incident. Some also may re-experience trauma as they learn new information related to the crime that only the offender can tell them.

> **Although the VOC process may be therapeutic for the victim or the offender, it is not therapy.**

Victims may have unrealistic expectations of how the offender will respond to hearing their story. Although the VOC process may be therapeutic for the victim or the offender, it is not therapy. Victims may be disappointed if the offender does not seem to understand the pain and anguish they have suffered.

Victims risk disappointment if the offender is unwilling or unable to provide adequate restitution or to follow through with agreements, or if the offender is not able to answer their questions.

Benefits for offenders

The traditional justice system rarely provides offenders the opportunity to face the real human costs of their actions. A dialogue with the victim helps offenders to better understand the implications of their offense in the victim's daily life.

Face-to-face encounters help offenders see victims as real people. For example, a person who burglarized a home may appreciate the fears that his victims and their children experienced after he invaded their privacy. Or, an offender may learn that the victims he had assumed to be wealthy in fact had needs very much like his own.

Encountering a victim and making restitution gives offenders the opportunity to "put things as right as possible." Some criminologists point out that much crime arises from feelings of rejection in the offender. Further rejection through imprisonment and labeling only increases the problem. Rarely are offenders given the opportunity to be reintegrated into the community.

VOC encourages offenders to take a role in their future instead of passively responding to decisions made for them. Thus, their sense of ownership of and commitment to fulfilling restitution often increases.

Finally, offenders have the opportunity to show that they are more than the crime they committed. They are not just a "monster"; they, too, are human. While the process acknowledges that the offender may have done something awful, this process also shows that the offender is not inherently bad.

Risks for offenders

Offenders often feel afraid about facing their victims, even in a controlled, safe setting. For many offenders, denying their victims' humanity is what enabled them to commit such crimes. To sit and listen to the pain victims experienced as a result of one's actions puts a human face to the crime. This is much different—and usually more difficult—than having to sit in a courtroom without ever conversing with the victims.

Offenders often fear that the victim will use this opportunity to exact revenge. They fear the victim will ask for an exorbitant amount of restitution or even physically threaten them once they sit down together in a room. Even when assured of a safe process, offenders usually find the encounter with the person they have harmed to be very difficult.

Research Summary

- 91 percent of offenders expressed satisfaction with the mediation process.

- For offenders, telling the victim what happened, apologizing, and paying restitution were important issues in the mediation process.

- Positive themes expressed by offenders include dealing with their feelings, correcting what was done, seeing victims change their attitude toward the offender, receiving a second chance, apologizing, and experiencing the mediation session as comfortable.[37]

Benefits for the community

Community-based programs empower communities to solve their own problems, reversing the tendency to look to others for solutions. Most VOC programs rely on community volunteers to facilitate this process, and, increasingly, to attend the conference as supportive participants.

A community's level of fear toward crime tends to decrease when they are part of creating a safer environment and helping to reduce various types of crime. The skills that trained facilitators learn are useful not only to resolve crime-related conflict but also for conflicts in other aspects of life. This may be particularly helpful in communities where victims and offenders are likely to meet again. The more the community is involved in the solution, the more likely it is invested in maintaining the relationships.

Another VOC benefit to the community is a reduction in recidivism. Offenders can avoid the damaging effects of incarceration, which often lead them to commit more crime. In addition, as offenders learn to see their victims as people and realize the human costs of crime, they are less likely to offend again.

Risks for the community

Some criminal justice systems may misuse VOC as a diversion technique from the traditional justice system because it is viewed as a quicker and cheaper method for disposing of cases. In such instances, VOC does not serve the community but the system.

Some members of the community also may view VOC as too soft on crime because it "lets the offender off the hook." If the community is not given an understanding of VOC's benefits and principles, or if it is not engaged in the process of designing and operating the program, VOC may be seen as an easy way out.

Research Summary

Most studies of juvenile victim offender programs have found that not only have youths re-offended less than youths in the control group but also that the crimes they committed tended to be less serious than the original offense.

Public opinion polls consistently show that the public prefers consequences that encourage offenders to make restitution and be accountable to victims and the community.[38]

Benefits for the legal system

VOC lessens the burden on courts and probation departments by providing a mechanism for establishing restitution amounts and agreements. This makes the option of restitution more attractive to the legal system without increasing its workload. Incidentally, the community also benefits by having VOC programs secure and oversee the restitution agreements, thereby saving time and resources.

VOC also provides an avenue for working with cases that are often insoluble in the criminal justice process, such as offenses involving neighborhood conflicts.

Finally, a successful VOC program can increase the legal system's credibility with victims and the community. VOC programs bring attention to victim needs, offender accountability, and community involvement that can increase the community's understanding of and support for criminal justice personnel.

Risks for the legal system

There is a danger that this process may become simply one more program to implement if 1) it is done by the system without ownership from the community, and 2) it is not part of a larger re-examination of the principles and practice of justice within the community. Without these aspects, adding VOC may increase the system's workload.

Research Summary

A 2007 research review looked at 36 studies from around the world that compared restorative justice and criminal justice approaches. Findings included the following:

- Restorative justice substantially reduces repeat offending for some offenders but not all. No study showed increased offending. Moreover, restorative justice more consistently reduces repeat offending with violent crimes than with less serious crimes.

- Crime victims who receive restorative justice tend to fare better, on average, in dealing with the trauma than victims who do not receive restorative justice. This applies to a wide range of outcomes, including post-traumatic stress.

- Restorative justice provides both victims and offenders more satisfaction with justice.

- Restorative justice exceeds the rate of compliance with court-ordered sanctions.

- When restorative justice is available, many more offenses can be brought to justice than when it is not. Diversion from prosecution to restorative justice substantially increases the odds of an offender being brought to justice.

- The evidence for restorative justice is far more extensive and positive than for many other national justice policies.

- Even if restorative justice has no effect on reducing crime, it is helpful to victims, where the evidence for restorative justice is compelling."[39]

Research on VOC is very promising. Satisfaction rates among both victims and offenders who participate are high. Victims' fears are reduced, offenders better understand the effects of their actions, and both victims and offenders have a better understanding of one another as individuals. Victims are more likely to receive restitution when agreements are made through victim offender encounters.[40]

To minimize risks, it is crucial that VOC programs be aware of these challenges and build in safeguards. These include active monitoring of restitution agreements until completion, and inviting victims and offenders and/or their service providers on VOC oversight boards to help maintain accountability to those they serve.

8.
Critical Issues in VOC

As noted in Chapter 7, research on the benefits of VOC is promising. However, there are challenges and pitfalls. Interventions are always susceptible to unintended consequences – unplanned and unforeseen outcomes. Any enthusiasm about VOC must be met with attention given to the dangers and challenges. The following briefly explores five such challenges.

1. VOC may be offender-driven.

In 1999-2000, restorative justice and victim advocates conducted a "Listening Project" to hear the concerns of victim advocates about restorative justice.[41] Although VOC practice claims to be victim-sensitive or even victim-oriented, in reality it may be driven by offender-related concerns. The following quote from the Listening Project captures this sentiment:

> Very often, restorative justice not only reflects offender needs – making amends, and changing and rehabilitating offenders – but is driven by such needs. Restorative justice may be offender-initiated, and may be oriented to an offender timeline.
> Such needs and practices may not be compatible with victim needs, however. Where offenders are provided with help to change their lives, but victims

are not provided help to deal with their trauma, victims feel betrayed by the offender orientation of restorative justice.[42]

The criticism from the victim community that victim offender processes are primarily driven by the offender and court timeline is a valid concern. An exception to this involves crimes of severe violence, in which dialogues are victim-initiated and generally happen well after the court process has been completed.

Because the traditional justice system is designed primarily to deal with offenders, any VOC initiatives must continually engage the victim community in partnership. They need to be an integral part of program planning and implementation.

VOC may help to address the needs of victims whose offenders are willing to meet, but what about victims whose offenders choose not to meet? How can victims' needs be met when a meeting is inappropriate or when offenders are unavailable or unwilling to meet with victims? It is

> **VOC initiatives must continually engage the victim community in partnership.**

important for VOC staff to remember these limitations and for the restorative justice field as a whole to provide services for victims where VOC is inappropriate or impractical.

Some programs have addressed this need by providing an opportunity for victims and offenders who are not from the same case to meet together. For example, an offender in a burglary case may agree to meet with a victim of a different burglary whose offender was unwilling to meet.

2. How do we (or should we) ensure appropriate voluntariness on the part of the offender in a victim offender process?

All VOCs stress the importance of fully voluntary participation on the part of victims. There is debate, however, about the extent to which offender participation is or should be voluntary. Most agree that coercing unwilling offenders into the process is counterproductive. It is also important for victims to know about any coercion so they can make an informed choice about their own participation. Programs need to ensure that victims are never coerced and must take steps to maximize the voluntary participation of offenders.

Eric Gilman discusses the Clark County (Washington) Juvenile Court commitment to respond restoratively to all victims and offenders:

> Beyond ethical considerations, there is little practical value in forcing someone to participate in any dialogue or mediation. If participants do not have some level of commitment to the dialogue process it is likely to be an unpleasant experience for everyone, including the facilitator/mediator, and likely a futile exercise as well. Participants in these encounters must see some potential value for themselves if they are going to meaningfully engage.
>
> Offenders must see potential benefit for themselves in order to be willing to participate in such a meeting. They need to see how a dialogue process can be of value to them. Being knowledgeable about issues important to offenders, and being able to connect those issues to a process of dialogue, is key to moving offenders to a place where they are willing to engage in a face-to-face meeting.[43]

3. Programs tend to be tied up intimately with the courts and police or prosecutors, who hold tremendous power over the processes.

Many VOC referrals come from the legal system, which might not refer certain cases. This can be a source of frustration when, for example, a victim or offender desires a VOC process and the system refuses. Or one offender in a multi-offender case may be referred and another not, again to the frustration of those involved. Moreover, the legal system reflects the structural problems of its community. Thus, patterns of racism and classism may influence the referral process and/or the outcomes the system accepts or imposes.

VOC programs need to be aware of these issues and work to resolve them. For example, the program is responsible to train facilitators on issues of oppression, and to work with the system to reduce the effects of these factors on cases. To do this, programs must have on their boards or accountability groups members of the social groups most affected by these policies.

Patterns of racism and classism may influence the referral process and/or the outcomes the system accepts or imposes.

It is also important for programs to provide opportunities for greater involvement at the community level. It's critical that community members see themselves as key stakeholders in the process, rather than as passive recipients of something done to or for them.

4. Current restorative justice approaches, such as VOC, tend to be individualistic in nature. How can these processes deal with community and social issues of harm?

In Chapter 1, Russ Kelly writes about his formative years and the loss of both parents by the time he was 15. He was unable to deal with the grief and trauma, and instead of finding healthy outlets to deal with his emotions, he turned to drugs and alcohol.

While his grief and loss do not excuse the behaviors he chose, his actions are quite common in such scenarios. VOC programs are designed to address the needs of victims and offenders as a result of one incident of harm, but many ask how it can address root causes rather than only the symptoms of crime. Restorative justice advocates and practitioners recognize this need to address the root causes and are implementing prevention approaches in communities, such as working with schools and at-risk youth.

5. VOC models, and the restorative justice concept that underlies them, contain important cultural biases.

The processes described in this *Little Book* were developed primarily within the context of a Western, Eurocentric framework. Critics point out that the facilitation styles may reflect this bias, and thus may not be appropriate for people from other traditions. Some have argued that basic assumptions underlying these practices and also the theory of restorative justice contain these unconscious biases.

One example of culturally-specific modifications made to programs is Morris Jenkins's work on Afrocentric restorative justice. Jenkins argues that Afrocentric and Eurocentric theory differ in four fundamental principles: cosmology (worldview), axiology (values), ontology (nature of people), and epistemology (source of knowledge).[44] He provides a "cultural justice model" that restorative justice practitioners could use in the African American community. He encourages practitioners to include alternative perspectives to enhance their current work.

VOC practitioners need to be as aware as possible about their own biases. They also must include and listen carefully to the perspectives of those from other traditions. Moreover, when implementing VOC in other cultures and societies, it must be adapted in a way that is appropriate to that context. Many cultures have existing traditions of resolving conflicts and harms that can be drawn upon. In these contexts, the "individualized" VOC model using "neutral" facilitators may be inappropriate.

Critics of VOC and restorative justice as a whole sometimes accuse advocates of telling "butterfly stories"—that is, collecting the best specimens to support their ideas. We can learn much from butterfly stories, and there are many available from the practice of VOC. But there are also cases that do not go well, and those who advocate for and practice VOC must learn from those stories as well.

Conclusion:
Moving Beyond Crime

My son and I were driving home together during one of his college breaks. He told me a story from his first year in college where, as he stated, he had put to good use the skills he had learned at home regarding conflict. He said that two of his friends were having a difficult time with each other, and he decided what they really needed was to sit in a room and talk it out. He sat them down together and told them no one was leaving the room until they had talked to each other about what was going on between them. He thought it went well.

I have to admit that I was squirming as my son told me about the process he used to work through the pain in his friends' relationship. Fortunately I held my thoughts in check and reminded myself that, even though some of his approaches weren't ones I might have used, they had apparently worked for him. Who gets to define restorative justice and its processes is a critical issue.

While I have provided a specific model with particular processes, I did so knowing that this is neither the only way nor the only right way. It is one way that comes from my particular worldview and context. As I learn to know and value the experiences that others bring to this work, my understanding of this practice continues to broaden. As these various experiences and worldviews merge within the practice of VOC, it becomes a more effective approach for all.

In the end, I was glad that my son recognized what restorative justice and VOC hold as central: that what matters are the relationships of individuals and their communities. These relationships must be at the core of any response.

I think VOC offers us that opportunity. It allows us to talk about harms and consequences in a way that strengthens communities and allows them to take care of themselves. This *Little Book* has applied these processes in the context of crime, but they have clear application to other areas of life as well.

Recommended Reading

Amstutz, Lorraine Stutzman and Howard Zehr. *Victim Offender Conferencing in Pennsylvania's Juvenile Justice System* (Commonwealth of Pennsylvania, 1998).

Liebmann, Marian. *Restorative Justice: How it Works* (London and Philadelphia: Jessica Kingsley Publishers, 2007).

MacRae, Allan and Howard Zehr. *The Little Book of Family Group Conferences: New Zealand Style* (Intercourse, PA: Good Books, 2004).

Umbreit, Mark S. *The Handbook of Victim Offender Mediation: An Essential Guide to Practice and Research* (San Francisco: Jossey-Bass, 2001).

Zehr, Howard. *The Little Book of Restorative Justice* (Intercourse, PA: Good Books, 2002).

Endnotes

1   For an overview of restorative justice, see Zehr, *The Little Book of Restorative Justice.*

2   Laura Mirsky, "Restorative Justice Practices of Native American, First Nation, and Other Indigenous People of North America: Part One," (International Institute for Restorative Practices, 2004) pp. 5-6. Available at http://www.realjustice.org/library/natjust1.html.

3   The complete story is available from Restorative Justice Online at http://www.restorativejustice.org/library/natjust1.html.

4   Mark Umbreit, et al., "National Survey of Victim-Offender Mediation Programs in the United States," (U.S. Department of Justice, April 2000) p. 3. Available at http://www.ojp.usdoj.gov.

5   Jim Shenk, "Mediator's Corner," in *Making Things Right* (Lancaster, PA: LAVORP, April 2002).

6   For more on Family Group Conferences, see MacRae and Zehr, *The Little Book of Family Group Conferences, New Zealand Style.*

7   Mark Umbreit, "Family Group Conferencing: Implications for Crime Victims," (U.S. Department of Justice, April 2000) p. 3. Available at http://www.ojp.usdoj.gov.

8   Lisa Merkel-Holguin, "Putting Families Back into the Child Protection Partnership: Family Group Decision Making," (American Humane, n.d.).

9   (Intercourse, PA: Good Books, 2005) p. 7.

10 Lorraine Stutzman Amstutz and Judy H. Mullett, *The Little Book of Restorative Discipline for Schools* (Intercourse, PA: Good Books, 2005) pp. 53-55.

[11] Napoleon, "By Whom, and By What Processes, Is Restorative Justice Defined, and What Bias Might This Introduce?" in *Critical Issues in Restorative Justice,* Howard Zehr and Barb Toews, eds., (Monsey, NY: Criminal Justice Press, 2004) p. 34.

[12] This story was written by Doris Luther, a VOC facilitator in Maine.

[13] Mark Umbreit, Betty Vos, and Robert Coates, "Restorative Justice Dialogue: Evidence-Based Practice," (Center for Justice & Peacemaking; University of Minnesota, Minneapolis, 2006). Available at http://rjp.umn.edu.

[14] Ibid.

[15] This story was provided by Shalom VORP of Northwest Ohio.

[16] Umbreit, *The Handbook of Victim Offender Mediation,* pp. 206-07.

[17] Ibid., p. 209.

[18] This story was provided by the Lancaster Area Victim-Offender Reconciliation Program. It was first printed in the "Mediator's Corner" column of the LAVORP newsletter.

[19] Amstutz and Zehr, *Victim Offender Conferencing in Pennsylvania's Juvenile Justice System,* pp. 45-55. Available online at http://www.mcc.org/us/peacebuilding under Print Resources.

[20] See "Victim-Offender Mediation Association Recommended Ethical Guidelines." Available at http://www.voma.org/docs/ethics.pdf.

[21] Ibid., p. 1.

[22] Shonna Robinson, victim/survivor, "The Beginning of a Healing Process," *Office of the Victim Advocate Newsletter* 4 (October 2000).

[23] Mark Umbreit, et al., "Executive Summary: Victim Offender Dialogue in Crimes of Severe Violence: A Multi-Site Study of Programs in Texas and Ohio," (Center for Restorative Justice & Peacemaking; University of Minnesota, Minneapolis, 2002) p. 2. Available at http://www.cehd.umn.edu/ssw/rjp under Resources.

24 Ibid.

25 See "Your Rights, Your Voice, Your Participation," from the Texas Department of Criminal Justice Victim Services Division. Available at http://www.tdcj.state.tx.us.

26 For more on the Ohio program, see Mark Umbreit, et al., *Facing Violence: The Path of Restorative Justice and Dialogue* (Monsey, NY: Criminal Justice Press, 2003).

27 Author's name withheld, "Real People, Real Stories: A Transforming Journey," in *Restorative Justice Online* (March 2006). Available online at http://www.restorativejustice.org/editions/2006/march06/victimstory.

28 Zehr, *The Little Book of Restorative Justice*, p. 19.

29 Ibid., pp. 22-24.

30 Ibid., p. 34.

31 Napoleon, "Restorative Justice Defined" in *Critical Issues in Restorative Justice*, p. 35.

32 Ibid.

33 Gilman, "Engaging Victims in a Restorative Process" (September, 2006) [p. 1]. Available at http://www.voma.org/docs/Engaging_Victims_in_a_Restorative_Process.pdf.

34 Sullivan and Tifft, "What Are the Implications of Restorative Justice for Society and Our Lives?" in *Critical Issues in Restorative Justice*, p. 388.

35 This discussion of risks and benefits is adapted from Amstutz and Zehr, *Victim Offender Conferencing in Pennsylvania's Juvenile Justice System*, pp. 26-29.

36 Mark Umbreit, Robert Coates, and Betty Vos, "Impact of Restorative Justice Conferencing with Juvenile Offenders: What We Have Learned from Two Decades of Victim Offender Dialogue Through Mediation and Conferencing," (Center for Restorative Justice & Peacemaking; University of Minnesota, Minneapolis, 2000).

37 Ibid.

38 Lawrence Sherman and Heather Strang, "Restorative Justice:
    The Evidence," (London: Smith Institute, 2007) p. 68. Available
    at http://www.smith-institute.org.uk/pdfs/RJ_full_report.pdf.

39 Ibid., p. 88.

40 Mark Umbreit, Robert Coates, and Betty Vos, "Victim-
    Offender Mediation" in *Handbook of Restorative Justice,*
    Dennis Sullivan and Larry Tifft, eds., (New York:
    Routledge, 2006).

41 Harry Mika, et al., "Taking Victims and Their
    Advocates Seriously: A Listening Project," (Akron, PA:
    Mennonite Central Committee, 2002) p. 5. Available at
    http://mcc.org/us/peacebuilding/print.html.

42 Ibid, p. 5.

43 Gilman, "Engaging Offenders in Restorative Dialogue
    Processes," (Clark County, Washington: Juvenile Court,
    September 2006). Available at http://www.voma.org/docs/
    Engaging_Offenders_in_Restorative_Dialogue.pdf.

44 Jenkins, "Afrocentric Restorative Justice," *VOMA Connections*
    20 (Summer 2005) p. 1. VOMA Newsletters are available at
    http://www.voma.org.

About the Author

Lorraine Stutzman Amstutz is Co-Director of Mennonite Central Committee's Office on Justice and Peacebuilding. She provides consulting and training for agencies and communities seeking to implement programs of restorative justice.

Lorraine has written numerous articles and co-authored *The Little Book of Restorative Discipline for Schools* (with Judy H. Mullet) and *Victim Offender Conferencing in Pennsylvania's Juvenile Justice System* (with Howard Zehr). She has served on the international Victim Offender Mediation Association (VOMA) Board as well as the local victim offender program in Lancaster County, PA. In 2007 she was awarded the Lancaster Mediation Center Peacemaker Award.

Lorraine received a bachelor's degree in Social Work from Eastern Mennonite University in Harrisonburg, VA, where she received the Distinguished Service Award for 2002. She earned a master's degree in Social Work from Marywood University, in Scranton, PA.

THE LITTLE BOOK OF

Family Group Conferences

NEW ZEALAND STYLE

Allan MacRae
& Howard Zehr

Table of Contents

Introduction

Allan: A story, but first some personal reflections

As I reflect on the Family Group Conferences I have facilitated, I am filled with emotion. These feelings come from the suffering I have witnessed but, more importantly, from the powerful processes of healing and forgiveness I have seen take place.

Having led over a thousand Family Group Conferences, I often find myself asking how anyone could cause such suffering for another person. As I facilitate Conferences where offenders hear the impact of their offending on victims and families, the answer becomes clear: even in attacks involving direct encounters with victims, offenders seldom realize the trauma they have inflicted. They do not grasp how difficult it is for victims to move on and to repair and reclaim their lives.

I have come to believe in Family Group Conferences because I have witnessed offenders having to face the impact they have had on people. I have seen healing come when they acknowledge the hurt they have caused, and when they struggle to correct what they can and take responsibility for what they cannot, through some form of compensation and apology.

The following story is about a 16-year-old boy who was charged with "rape times three" on the same victim, a 13-year-old girl. This story demonstrates how Conferences can deal with serious and complicated cases, and the power of practice based in principle.

As is so often the case, the offender—I'll call him Robert—had himself been the victim of pedophiles from the age of five. His mother would take him to meetings of pedophiles and participate in their activities. In short, this was a boy who had not experienced appropriate sexual boundaries.

Joanne, his victim, had also been a victim previously. Having been subjected to incest, she found only one method of coping within her power. She shut down when under attack, allowing her mind to escape her body as best she could.

Robert and Joanna both ended up living in the same home as longer-term plans were being made for their care. Before long, Robert approached Joanna in her room. When he made sexual advances, Joanna responded the only way she knew; she closed down. When he didn't receive physical or verbal rejection, Robert returned twice more, although it was clear that he had not received any encouragement.

When I visited Joanna to explain her rights, I did so with the support of her caregiver and social worker. After hearing her rights, Joanna said she wanted to view the Conference but not be in the same room as the offender. I arranged for the Conference to be held in one room while she watched it through a video monitor in the next room. I suggested that she may want to have a representative in the room with the offender to speak for her. Joanna proposed that her caregiver represent her in the Conference while she observed from outside with an adult woman friend and her social worker.

The event was held over two evenings; much information was given to the Conference participants to prepare them for the many decisions they would need to make. During the meetings, Joanna sent three powerful letters from outside the room for her representative to read to the Conference participants. In the first letter she directly challenged Robert, the offender, saying that he was not taking enough responsibility for what happened. As a result, Robert apologized and took full responsibility. In the second letter she stated that she did not want Robert to lose his job so that he could pay for the self-defense lessons she wanted to take. In the third letter she expressed her concern that she not run into him while she was in the early stages of her recovery. She stated that she did not want him to come to the area where she lived and visited, including where she socialized on Friday and Saturday nights, even if he was under escort.

The Conference worked out a plan that met all of Joanna's requests. Robert would not lose his job, but he was not allowed to leave his place of work for any reason unless under escort. He was to be transported to and from his place of work each day. The plan required him to be under 24-hour supervision until he had completed a program for sexual offenders. All the conditions Joanna asked for, including 24-hour supervision, were to be made conditions of bail for a minimum of six months. This meant that Robert could be arrested immediately if found in breach of his bail. The plan called for Robert to be placed under the guardianship of the Director General of Social Welfare until he was 19. In turn, the police agreed that the charges could be amended to be an unlawful sexual connection, a lesser charge.

In short, the Conference developed a plan that met the needs of the victim and placed the offender into an extended program to minimize the immediate and long-term risks to the community. The offender would be held accountable, and his legal expenses were minimized.

On the day following the event, I phoned the caregiver to see how Joanna was coping in the aftermath. The caregiver said, "It's absolutely amazing. When we got home last night, Joanna walked in the door and said, 'I don't need to wear this coat anymore.' She slipped it off her shoulders and let it drop to the floor." Joanna had worn the coat ever since she was abused. The day after the Conference met, "She was present in a different way than I had ever seen her before. She looked as if an incredible weight had been lifted from her, and she was full of smiles and energy."

Robert completed all his obligations, including giving the police a DNA sample and paying for Joanna's self-defense classes. He stayed under supervision and finished the long-term plan under the care and protection status within the guardianship of Social Welfare. He faced the fact that he did not have the right to victimize others, while acknowledging that he needed help to live successfully and positively within the community.

This plan pushed boundaries: typically the boy would have gone to jail. And that would likely have led to his committing further offenses, eventually destroying any hope of his living successfully within the community. The potential outcome of this case was so groundbreaking that the police were not willing to shoulder responsibility for it alone. They wanted a judge to take that responsibility. The judge agreed, and she was given no cause for regret.

At the end of the first six months Robert was discharged from the Youth Court because he had successfully completed his agreement. Joanna, although only 13 years old, was a very strong person who used the Conference to meet her own needs for healing.

Through this case, I learned that even very young victims need to have a voice, that over-protection can be disempowering. A young person like Joanna can know what she needs for her own well-being and can initiate healing through the Conference process.

Allan and Howard: About this book

Family Group Conferences like this one are the primary forum in New Zealand for dealing with serious youth crime, as well as child welfare issues. This book is about this decision-making process in the youth justice arena, the Conferences (known as "FGCs") themselves, but also the juvenile justice system that is built around these Conferences.

Since their introduction in New Zealand in 1989, Family Group Conferences (sometimes with other names such as "community group conferences" or "community accountability conferences") have been adopted and adapted in many places throughout the world. They have been used as decision-making processes in many arenas, including child welfare, school discipline, and criminal justice, both juvenile and adult. In fact, Family Group Conferences have emerged as one of the most promising models of restorative justice.

There are, however, several different forms of FGCs. The most widely known model is based on an Australian adaptation; this model has strongly influenced the approach used by the Thames Valley Police in the United Kingdom, the Royal Canadian Mounted Police, and that of many communities in North America. New Zealand's method has some distinctive and important features that deserve consideration. It is the original model and the source of the term "Family Group Conference."

This *Little Book of Family Group Conferences* is designed to provide an introduction to FGCs, New Zealand style. We will describe the overall approach and provide information about how an FGC is conducted. Although this is not a complete how-to manual, it does provide many of the basics, especially when used in conjunction with other restorative justice material such as *The Little Book of Restorative Justice* or other material like that listed in the Appendices. And while some of the information is specific to New Zealand, much about the approach can be and has been adapted to many other settings.

Having said that, we do want to caution against simple replication of the model. New Zealand's FGCs are deliberately designed to allow individual Conferences to be adjusted to the cultures of those who participate. Nevertheless, no model should simply be copied and plugged into another context. We urge you to take from this what fits, to adapt it as necessary to your own setting. In doing so, however, we emphasize the importance of dialogue, of listening to each other, especially to the "stakeholders" (those most impacted by the crime), and to indigenous and minority groups in your community. Moreover, we cannot emphasize enough the importance of grounding practice in principle. We suggest the concept of restorative justice as a starting point for a discussion of principles.

Introduction

A few words, yet, about the authors[1] of this book. Allan MacRae is currently the Manager of Coordinators for the Southern Region of New Zealand, overseeing Family Group Conferences for both Youth Justice, and Care and Protection. Prior to taking this position, he was Youth Justice Coordinator for the capital city of Wellington. This *Little Book* draws upon and systematizes his experience there. When the pronoun "I" is used it refers to Allan.

Co-author Howard Zehr, Co-Director of the Conflict Transformation Program at Eastern Mennonite University (Harrisonburg, Virginia), is considered one of the founders of the field of restorative justice and is often called upon to interpret restorative justice in various parts of the world. He has frequently lectured and consulted in New Zealand.

Over a number of years of teaching together, visiting each other, and fishing together, we—Allan and Howard —have become friends. By combining our perspectives and talents, we hope to translate the practice of FGCs into a form that will be helpful to you.

---

[1] Allan MacRae passed away in January 2015, shortly before this edition was compiled. He served New Zealand's Child, Youth and Family system for 34 years. Howard Zehr has retired from teaching but continues part-time as Distinguished Professor of Restorative Justice and Co-Director of the Zehr Institute for Restorative Justice at Eastern Mennonite University.

1.
An Overview

During the 1980s, New Zealand faced a crisis familiar to other Western nations around the world. Thousands of children, especially members of minority groups, were being removed from their homes and placed in foster care or institutions. The juvenile justice system was overburdened and ineffective. New Zealand's incarceration rate for young people was one of the highest in the world, but its crime rate also remained high. At the same time, New Zealand's punitive approach was also in part a "welfare" model. Although young people were being punished, they were also being rewarded by receiving attention. Yet they were not being required to address the actual harm they had caused.

Especially affected was the minority Maori population, the indigenous people of New Zealand. Maori leaders pointed out that the Western system of justice was a foreign imposition. In their cultural tradition, judges did not mete out punishment. Instead, the whole community was involved in the process, and the intended outcome was repair. Instead of focusing on blame, they wanted to know "why," because they argued that finding the cause of crime is part of resolving it. Instead of punishment ("Let shame be the punishment" is a Maori proverb), they were concerned with healing and problem-solving. The Maori also pointed out that the Western system, which undermined the family and disproportionately incarcerated Maori youth, emerged from a larger pattern of institutional racism. They argued persuasively that cultural identity is based on three primary institutional pillars—law, religion, and education—and when any of these undermines or ignores the values and traditions of the indigenous people, a system of racism is operating.

Because of these concerns, in the late 1980s the government initiated a process of listening to communities throughout the country. Through this listening process, the Maori recommended that the resources of the extended family and the community be the source of any effort to address these issues. The FGC process emerged as the central tool to do this in the child protection and youth justice systems.

> **FGCs are intended to empower and value participants, while building upon the resources of the extended family and community.**

In 1989 the legislature passed a landmark Act of Parliament. The Children, Young Persons and Their Families Act totally revamped the focus and process of juvenile justice in New Zealand. Although it did not use this terminology until later, the New Zealand legal system became the first in the world to institutionalize a form of restorative justice. Family Group Conferences became the hub of New Zealand's entire juvenile justice system. In New Zealand today, an FGC, not a courtroom, is intended to be the normal site for making such decisions.

The Conference

FGCs are a kind of decision-making meeting, a face-to-face encounter involving offenders and their families, victims and their supporters, a police representative, and others. Organized and led by a Youth Justice Coordinator, a facilitator who is a social services professional, this approach is designed to support offenders as they take responsibility and change their behavior, to empower the offenders' families to play an important role in this process, and to address the victims' needs. Unlike restorative justice programs attached to justice systems elsewhere, this group together formulates the *entire outcome* or disposition, not just restitution. Importantly—and remarkably—they do this by *consensus* of all the participants, not by a mere majority or the decree of an official. Victim, offender, family members, youth advocate, or police can individually block an outcome if one of them is unsatisfied.

Particular Characteristics of New Zealand FGCs

- **intended for serious offenses**
- **the hub of the entire system**
- **governed by principles**
- **deals with the entire outcome**
- **uses consensus decision-making**
- **family-centered**
- **offers a family caucus**
- **aims at cultural adaptability and appropriateness**

Although there are similar elements in most Conferences, FGCs are intended to be adapted to the needs and perspectives of the participants. One of the goals of the process is to be *culturally appropriate,* and another is that it should *empower families.* It is the job of the coordinator to help the families determine who should be present and to design a process that will be appropriate for the needs and traditions of those involved.

Thus, there is not a scripted model in which the facilitator follows a predetermined text. While there is often a common overall pattern to Conferences, each is to be adapted to the situation. An element common to most Conferences, however, is a family caucus sometime during the event. Here the offender and family are left alone to discuss what has happened and to develop a proposal to bring back to the victim and the rest of the Conference.

Like the facilitator in other forms of restorative justice encounters, the coordinator of an FGC must seek to be impartial, balancing the concerns and interests of all parties. However, he or she is charged with making sure a plan is developed that addresses causes as well as reparation, that holds the offender adequately accountable, and that is realistic. The facilitator also must make sure that the Conference addresses issues of follow-up and monitoring. Who is to do what and when, and who is to monitor this, are all part of the plan that emerges from an FGC.

The system

In New Zealand, Family Group Conferences are not only a kind of meeting or encounter, they are the hub of an entire youth justice system.

Most countries and communities which employ restorative justice programs—FGCs or otherwise—use such programs or Conferences on a case-by-case basis, at the discretion of the legal system. The courtroom is the norm, and restorative justice is an add-on or diversion from it. In New Zealand, however, the Family Group Conference is the norm, and the courtroom is the backup.

An FGC is both a Conference and a justice system.

The system is designed so that all of the more serious juvenile cases are to be referred to an FGC, with the exception of murder and manslaughter. In New Zealand, a special branch of the police—Youth Aid Officers—are designated to work with young people. They work at prevention and law enforcement, but also serve as the prosecution, deciding what charges to file or "lay." This is why these officers must be present at an FGC, since the FGC will together decide what charges will ultimately be filed, or whether all charges should be dropped. The police have a significant role in deciding whether a case will go to an FGC or will be disposed of without such a Conference.

More minor offenses—about 80% of juvenile crimes that come to the attention of the police—are intended to be handled by the police through "cautioning" and release (in the U.S., these are sometimes called "reprimand and release"), or through diversionary approaches such as informal victim-offender mediation.

When an accused young person denies a charge but it is proven in Court, the case must go back to an FGC who will recommend to the Court how the proven charge should be addressed. Even though a Conference would not be held to address murder or manslaughter charges, a Conference may still be required to address custody issues while the offender awaits trial or sentencing. The Conference would consider alternatives to custody, or what should be provided to the young person while in custody, such as cultural, religious, or other needs or wishes of the family. This Conference could also recommend who is allowed to visit the young person while in custody.

New Zealand law identifies four types of youth justice Family Group Conferences. **"Custody Conferences"** must be held when a young person is placed in custody after denying the charge. **"Charge Proven Conferences"** are called for by a court when a young person has denied guilt but is then found guilty in court. **"Intention to Charge Conferences"** (the young person is not arrested, but is referred directly to a Youth Justice Coordinator for a Conference) decide if a child or young person should be prosecuted, or how the matter can be dealt with in another way. **"Charge Not Denied Conferences"** (the young person is arrested and brought before the court) are directed by the court (as soon as the young person admits responsibility for what has occurred) to recommend one of the following—the charges should be removed from court; a plan for addressing the charges; amendments to the charges; how the court should dispose of the matter.

Most FGCs, then, are not intended to involve courts significantly. Only when Conferences are held to make sentence recommendations, or when a Conference recommends some court monitoring or enforcement, is there to be oversight by the court. On occasion, a court-ordered Conference recommends that the charges be withdrawn from the court to promote less formal monitoring. This can only happen when the police agree, when the police and other Conference participants

Youth Justice Process

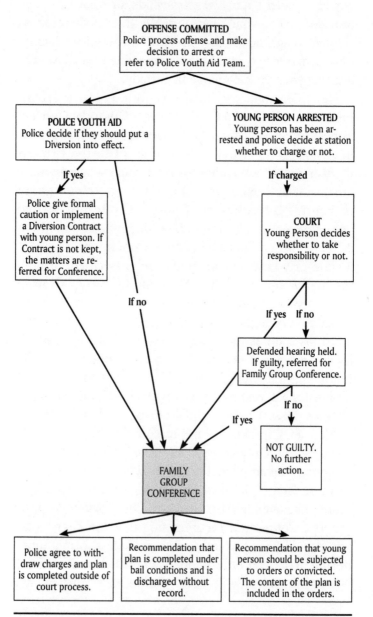

have confidence that the plan will be completed, and when the perpetrator shows genuine remorse.

Judge Fred McElrea, a prominent New Zealand judge and advocate of restorative justice, argues that this approach appropriately makes the community, not the court, the center of decision-making. Not only has the number of young people appearing in court in New Zealand dropped, but less court time is needed to deal with them. Consequently, the court can focus on safeguarding the process and dealing with special cases.

On page 220 is a simplified flowchart providing an overview of the process or system.

2.
Principled Practice

The cornerstone of the youth justice system in New Zealand is the Family Group Conference. The system works because all elements, from the police through the courts, are guided by principles and goals established in the 1989 Act. There are numerous examples of practitioners straying from these principles and goals. But if they are followed—if the goals and principles are regularly used in designing and running Conferences—they will lead to restorative practice. *In our opinion, these clear goals and principles, and cultivated habits of referring to them in making decisions, will result in good practice and, ultimately, a restorative approach.*

Seven goals

The seven primary goals of youth justice in New Zealand can be summarized like this:

- **Diversion**—A key goal is to keep young people out of the courts and to prevent labeling them as offenders. Underlying this are several assumptions: a) contact with the criminal justice system often increases, rather than decreases, offending; b) most youthful offending is developmental rather than pathological, so most offenders will grow out of it;

and c) community-based sanctions can focus better on needs and behaviors than custodial ones can.

- **Accountability**—Offenders must be held accountable and thus encouraged to accept responsibility for their actions and to repair the harm they have caused. This concept is explored further in the principles below.

- **Involving the victim**—Victims' needs must be addressed, and victims themselves must have an opportunity to be part of deciding the outcomes. Victim involvement also provides genuine accountability for offenders.

- **Involving and strengthening the offender's family**—The offender's family should be involved in the processes and outcomes. It is needed to encourage its young person to make good decisions and to provide the resources to carry them out. An important underlying assumption is that families, even fragmented or dysfunctional ones, are able to help their young people work through the effects of their behavior if they give them support.

- **Consensus decision-making**—Outcomes should be agreed upon by all participants, not imposed by a majority or "from above."

- **Cultural appropriateness**—Processes and assistance should be adapted to the cultural perspectives and needs of the participants.

- **Due process**—The young person's rights must be respected. Specialized "youth advocates" are appointed to assist in the process and to watch that these rights are observed.

Seven guiding principles

To achieve these goals, the 1989 Act spells out seven guiding principles for the Family Group Conference process in youth justice cases. These principles apply not only to the FGC process, but to all youth justice procedures in New Zealand.

- *Criminal proceedings should be avoided unless the public interest requires otherwise.* The system, including FGCs, does need to consider public interest.

  In practice, this means that the coordinator needs to come to the FGC with the information needed to consider alternatives. The presence of a police representative ensures that public interest factors are not overlooked.

- *Criminal justice processes should not be used to provide assistance.* Criminal proceedings should not be used to address welfare needs such as protection, residence, or care.

  Prior to the 1989 Act, the "welfare approach" had often used criminal proceedings to try to meet the welfare needs of young people. This resulted in unnecessary charges and increased rates of institutionalization.

- *Families should be strengthened.* The Act specifies that any measures taken should be designed to: 1) strengthen the family group; and 2) foster the ability of the family to develop its own means of dealing with offending within the family.

  Most parents of misbehaving children feel helpless. Parents are often confused about their options and the resources available to help. Typical justice responses, which commonly shift matters from parents to professionals, increase the parents' sense of helplessness and frustration. Justice responses, then, should be designed to help the family deal with its own problems.

When an FGC is convened, it is important to ensure that the assailant's family has the appropriate networks to allow the FGC plan to succeed. The first preference is to enlist the support of extended family, but, where this is not available or sufficient, creating a community of support around the family is the next best option.

The Act assumes—and subsequent experience confirms—that when families are encouraged to "put things right" with the victim(s) and community, and given support to do so, the results are more effective. When the family develops its own plans for reparation, its members have greater ownership and commitment to make the FGC reparation plan work. An additional advantage of the FGC process is that youth offenders' siblings witness the modeling of accountability, responsibility, and reparation. This is a form of prevention.

- *Children should be kept in the community if at all possible.* Research has shown that young offenders feel isolated within their communities. In Wellington, the capital city of New Zealand, most youth who offend are Samoans and Maori who live outside their tribal areas or Caucasians who have been separated from their support networks by a family split or an employment relocation by their parents.

  Removing youths from their natural communities only adds to their feeling of not belonging, which can lead to their losing respect for their current communities. If youths do not respect or feel unjustly treated by their communities, if they do not feel they belong, it is easier for them to offend against them.

Young people who were raised outside a family environment have little experience on which to base their own parenting skills. Those who have had extended periods in residential or institutional care also lack the skills to socialize and to develop support networks within their communities. Gangs and subcultures pick them up. In fact, incarceration contributes to the problem by making many youths feel angry towards society, creating within them a strong feeling of not belonging and preventing them from developing the very skills they need for positive change.

- *The child or young person's age must be taken into account.* Youth are still developing, and decision-makers should remember that a young person's behavior and needs are profoundly affected by this process. Except for murder and manslaughter, young people under the age of 17 normally go to an FGC, not a court, where decisions are made about their overall needs and responsibilities.

- *Personal development should be promoted using the least restrictive option.* This principle, which overlaps with those above, says that: 1) any sanctions should be designed to promote the development of the young person within his or her family group; and 2) within those circumstances, the least restrictive form that is appropriate should be taken. One of the reasons for this principle is that children and youth have a strong sense of justice. Overly restrictive responses offend that sense of justice, which every community should be enhancing in its youth.

- *The interests of victims must be considered.* This principle reminds practitioners that victims are an essential part of the equation. Justice must provide an opportunity for victims to be involved, to help define their own needs, and to have their needs addressed.

The "interests of victims" principle exists for the sake of victims, but also for the sake of offenders. It is very effective to have young people focus on the impact of their actions. They gain a clear understanding of what they have done and how they can correct the impact to the best of their abilities. Unlike punishment, this is true accountability since it has natural and logical consequences.

In processes where the offender is held accountable to *the state,* s/he has very little connection to the offense, the victim, the family, or the community where the offense occurred. Any punitive conse-

Seven Goals	Seven Principles
• diversion • accountability • victim involvement • family empowerment • consensus decision-making • cultural appropriateness • due process	• avoid criminal proceedings • don't use justice for assistance • strengthen families • keep offenders in community • take age into account • use least restrictive option • consider victim interests

quence for the offense is viewed by the youth as an act of vengeance by the community and further contributes to her/his isolation. This does not help the offender understand the real impact of what s/he has done.

The Family Group Conference places priority on the victim's needs, which may include financial settlement as partial reparation. The FGC gives the victim a voice, and this can be healing to both the victim and the youth who has offended. When young persons complete their commitments to the victims, they often feel better about themselves. This in turn contributes toward a more positive lifestyle. Recidivism research suggests that offenders who have put things right are less likely to re-offend. So when youth are held accountable in a restorative manner, there is a greater chance of a satisfactory outcome for victims, for offenders, and for the community.

Since 1989, the practice of FGCs in New Zealand has varied in quality. In some areas the approach has been highly successful. Where it has not lived up to its potential, we believe it is because of a failure to use and follow these principles and goals consistently. Where the Youth Justice system has been successful, these principles and goals have been used not only to shape policy, but also to guide decisions in each case and each situation.

Again, we point to the importance of goals and principles for guiding good practice. Although standards of practice and ethical guidelines can be helpful, we suggest that clear principles and goals are even more important. We strongly encourage any community that is designing restorative or conflict-resolution processes to establish appropriate goals and principles. Having done that, be sure to draw on culturally-appropriate values as you use those goals and principles as a guide to practice.

3.
Organizing a Family Group Conference

New Zealand law establishes different kinds of Family Group Conferences for child offenders and youth offenders. FGCs held for child offenders (between 10 and 14 years old) primarily focus on the welfare and interests of the child more than on the offending behavior as such. Here the well-being of the child is paramount, but that is, of course, coupled with obligations to teach the child accountability and responsibility. Youth offenders (those between 14 and 17 years old), on the other hand, can be held criminally accountable. Regardless of the type, the basic shape of the FGC process is the same. The following is a description of the roles involved and how a Conference is put together and conducted.

The Coordinator's role

The person who organizes and oversees the overall process, and normally facilitates the Conference itself, is called a Youth Justice Coordinator.

The Coordinator receives reports from the police and meets with them to explore alternatives to filing criminal charges. Indeed, collaboration with the police is a key element in communities where the Youth Justice system has been especially effective in reducing crime. In fact, in an effort to increase collaboration, a recent focus in New Zealand is on creating "youth offending teams" which comprise all of the professionals involved in Youth Justice.

Once it has been decided to take a case to an FGC, the Coordinator's tasks are to:
1) prepare the parties,
2) convene and facilitate the Conference,
3) monitor the principles of the Act,
4) record the agreements or plans, and
5) communicate the results to the appropriate people and agencies.

More specifically, the Coordinator is required to:
a. Consult with the offender and the *family* of the offender about:
   - the process to be used in the FGC, and the date, time, and venue for the FGC and,
   - who should be invited. Under New Zealand law, the offender's extended family members are entitled to attend the FGC, so it is important to consult with the family about what additional support they may require.

b. Consult with the *victim* about:
   - whether s/he wishes to attend and, if so, the date, time, and venue for the FGC, and,
   - his/her rights in the process. This includes the different ways in which s/he can participate in the process. Victims may send a representative, have phone contact with the FGC, write letters, or have the FGC Coordinator put information

through to the FGC on his/her behalf. This information may be presented as a video or audio tape or simply be conveyed as a verbal message. If the victim or a representative does attend, that person is entitled to have support people come along. The victim may decline to participate at all. Good support for victims encourages them to attend and to receive benefit from the Conference. Research shows that the best results are achieved when victims attend, but it must be their choice to do so.

c. Take all reasonable steps to give notification, including date, time, and venue, of the Family Group Conference to all those who are entitled to attend.

d. Find out the views of those persons who are involved but are unable to attend the Family Group Conference.

e. Ensure that relevant information and advice is made available to the Family Group Conference that will enable the FGC to carry out its functions. This includes providing information about services and networks in the community that may be relevant. The Coordinator needs to have a well-functioning network within the community and with other professionals.

f. Convene and guide the Conference itself, adapting it to the cultural setting and to the needs of the parties.

g. Ensure that the decisions, recommendations, and plans which emerge are within the principles that guide the process.

h. Record the decisions, recommendations, or plans made by the Family Group Conference and ensure that they are made available to the appropriate persons and agencies (such as the police and court). If the plans require the service of an agency or a person who is not present at the FGC, the Coordinator must seek that entity's agreement after the FGC.

i. Reconvene the FGC if two people who attended the FGC request it, the plan calls for it, the Court orders it, or if the Coordinator or police feel there is a need to reconvene the FGC (e.g., if parts are not working).

As a facilitator, the Coordinator's role includes something similar to mediation. As the multiple task list above suggests, however, the term "mediation" is not totally appropriate. Like a mediator, the Coordinator must seek to be impartial and balanced and may not impose outcomes or solutions. However, the Coordinator is responsible for helping the police or courts make decisions about the process, ensuring that the offender is held adequately accountable during the Conference, and seeing that the plan adopted by the FGC is manageable, appropriate, and monitored. In short, the Coordinator is mandated to ensure that the process and outcomes are guided by the principles.

Conference participants

In addition to the Coordinator, the Youth Justice System in New Zealand makes provision for the following participants in an FGC. However, attendance is only mandated for offenders, family members of the offenders, and police representatives.

- *Offenders and their families,* including extended family,

- *Victims or victim representatives,* and supporters,

- *Police representatives* (Youth Aid Officer),

- *Youth Advocates.* Special lawyers are carefully selected and appointed to assist in Youth Justice cases. They are to safeguard the rights of the young offenders and assist the process; their role is not adversarial.

- *Lay Advocates.* These may be appointed to advise on cultural matters, to help make sure the process is culturally appropriate for those involved.

- *Social workers* can attend if the young offender's family wishes, or if the agency has legal custody, guardianship, or supervision, or if it is required to give support to the child/young person.

- *Information-givers.* In some cases, someone with special information (e.g., community, school, or church representatives) may attend, but only for the relevant part of the Conference.

- Other *care-givers,* i.e., any person currently having care of the offending child or young person.

Preparation

Let's assume that you are a Youth Justice Coordinator charged with putting together an FGC, New Zealand style.

Begin the process by sending letters to the victims, the offender, and the offender's parents. These letters should include a pamphlet explaining the process and should ask the recipients to contact the Coordinator within 72 hours. Use the written word only to open the opportunity to communicate or to confirm an agreement that has been reached.

If you have not heard from recipients of the letters within a few days (in New Zealand, short statutory time limits of two to three weeks are placed on the process), follow up with a phone call. On the phone, ask to meet with them to explain their rights and options in more detail. Most people agree to a meeting in their home. Here are some observations and suggestions growing out of our experience as practitioners:

• Person-to-person communications are more likely to build rapport and understanding than phone or letter contact. When you communicate in this way you receive the benefit of full interaction. Real communication includes listening to the tone of someone's voice and a visual observation of body language. For example, people may say they will attend the FGC, especially the victim or the victim's associates, but their body language tells you they are not feeling comfortable with that decision. By acknowledging their apparent discomfort, you can open a discussion about their level of comfort and address the issues that cause it. Experience has shown that unless the discomfort is addressed, people usually decide at the last minute not to attend.

• The next best form of communication is by phone. It is important, though, to try first to meet the victim or associate face-to-face. Experience shows that the percentage of Conferences with victims attending is significantly higher when victims are invited in person. So even if victims may express on the phone that they do not wish to attend the FGC, ask if they would be willing to meet with you so you can explain their rights in the FGC process. Most

> **Victims may**
>
> - attend all or part,
> - decline to participate,
> - send representatives,
> - send information.

agree to meet with the Coordinator, and then end up attending the Conference.

• The written word is the most unreliable form of communication. Letters and emails are often misunderstood. Do not rely on letters or email as a sole form of communication.

• Good communications skills are required by anyone facilitating a Family Group Conference process. The facilitator needs to be able to explain the process, negotiate and seek agreements, guide the meetings, and record the decisions accurately. The facilitator's communication skills need to function well in a number of situations, including the FGC, meetings with the enforcement agencies, and the court.

Working with victims

The initial reason for meeting with victims is to inform them of their rights and to give them information about the process. Although it is preferable to have them at the Conference, and usually beneficial to them, it is inappropriate to pressure them into attending.

In New Zealand, victims have the right to participate in three ways. First, they have the right to be present and to bring support people with them. This could be a family member, close friend, caregiver, or a representative of a victim support organization. Second, they may send a representative, and that person may bring support people. Third, victims may choose to send information only. In this third option, however, they do not have a right to object to or disagree with the outcome of the Conference, although they can refuse any outcome that involves them directly. This could include a personal apology or work done by the offender for them.

You should first consult with the victims on the date, time, and venue for the Conference. Because the victims are being asked to give their time to attend an FGC, share information that may help them decide the value of giving that time. Often victims fear re-victimization, and it is helpful to be able to tell them that the Conference process is designed to safeguard against this. Other factors to share are the successes that are being achieved through the FGC process. Some examples of these achievements are in the Appendices (pages 273-276).

The majority of victims choose to attend, but some require assistance, like travel, babysitters, or compensation for the loss of income. The New Zealand system normally provides some financial assistance for such needs. To accommodate work schedules, FGCs are often held in the evenings.

Again, it is important for you as Coordinator to be flexible about how victims wish to be involved, to support their needs, and to ensure that they choose how they want to participate. Present all the options with as much information as possible so victims can make an educated decision that best suits them. Whether victims choose to be involved or not, it is important that victims' interests be taken into account in Conference plans.

There are a number of ways that a victim can participate without actually being in the Conference. The Coordinator may share information on the victim's behalf or the victim can choose to send a video or audio message to be played during the Conference. A victim may participate by phone for whole or part of the Conference or can choose to observe the Conference through a closed-circuit video link and be supported in another room by a social worker and other persons. Notes written by the victim can be read to the offender and the Conference as a whole. All of these ways help to insure that the victim's wishes are included in the plan.

Victims or their representatives should know that they have a choice as to whether to participate in the full Conference or only in part of it. The latter usually means the victim will attend the information-sharing part of the Conference. (That usually precedes the private deliberations between the offender and his/her family.)

In most cases, if the victim is not going to remain for the full Conference, the offender's family gives the victim assurance that they will include the victim's wishes in the final plan, and the Coordinator agrees to monitor this.

Victims may also choose to become involved at a planned reconvening of the FGC, when the offending child or youth has demonstrated some commitment and taken steps to " put things right."

In some cases, such as traffic offenses or drug charges, there is no identifiable victim. In these cases the community is considered the victim, and police represent the community. However, it would be possible to involve surrogate victims as information-givers, such as those who have suffered from drunk driving or drug use. But it must be remembered that they cannot be there as entitled participants, nor do they have the right to remain for the whole Conference, or to agree or disagree with the plan. There is the risk that they may expect the young person to put right what happened to them.

As Coordinator, you should explain the process to the victim, as well as the fact that you are consulting with the offender and the offender's family. Since New Zealand law allows and encourages the offender and family to take responsibility for shaping the process, you may need to check back with the victim about special process requests the offender may make. If there are cultural differences, you may need to negotiate between the parties about such things as the use of prayers, as discussed below.

You should also inform victims that they are entitled to tell the offender how angry they are and how the offense has affected them. They may ask questions as well. Make clear that they should not agree to the plan which will outline how the young person will be held accountable unless they feel it is fair and just. Explain that the FGC is not about debating the offender's guilt with the victim, since the FGC can only make decisions affecting the child or young person if the charge is admitted or proven in court.

When working with victims, offenders, and their families, it is important to ask whether they wish to start the Conference with a prayer or blessing, or whether there are other cultural protocols they would like to have incorporated. For many Maori, South Pacific, and other regional groups, a prayer is culturally very important. Encourage them to say a prayer if they wish to do so and to use their customary language and traditions. It is the Coordinator's responsibility to inform both "sides"—victims as well as offenders—of these wishes so they know what to expect. You may need to do some back-and-forth communication between victim and offender families to determine a process that is appropriate for both. You may also need to provide translators for either or both parties.

Working with offender and family

The first piece of conflict resolution work is facilitating the convening of the Conference (date, time, venue, who will attend) and ensuring that victims' interests are looked after in the process the Conference will follow. The Co-ordinator is required to consult with the offending child/ young person's family about those same details and the process the FCG will follow.

It is important early on to check the offender's—and his/her family's—understanding of the charge. If there are discrepancies or misunderstandings, ask the police and the youth's advocate (lawyer) to clarify them.

Because many families are entering the process for the first time, explain that the law entitles them to have private deliberation time (the family caucus) and that the family's deliberations usually divide the Conference into three main parts or phases (as explained later in this chapter).

Advise the offender's family that their decision-making is critical because the FGC gives a clear priority to young offenders who are held accountable within the support of their extended families. The FGC process should enable their best decision-making.

Once the family has an understanding of the FGC process and of their own responsibilities, ask for a list of people they would like to invite as support. It is important to clarify that "family" is to be broadly interpreted and should include anyone who can assist in putting a plan together or in helping to resource it.

Often the child/young person has someone s/he looks up to. If so, that person should be included in the FGC. A young offender can be greatly encouraged by having someone s/he respects helping to put things right, and to do so with a positive attitude. This person can also act as an advocate for the child/young person because an offense often puts a strain on the child/young person's relationship with his/her family. This is especially true when a family member is the victim, e.g., an assault on a parent. Advise the family that other adults who are outside the family, but have a positive relationship with their child/young person, may also be of assistance; perhaps a team coach, youth group leader, minister, or teacher.

If the family does not have extended networks, it is important to assist them in developing such support. For this purpose, the Coordinator needs to be well connected in the community. Coordinators ought to create working relationships with a number of organizations from different cultures and with different resources. These organizations can offer venues and support for families. It is not uncommon for these organizations also to be contracted to monitor an outcome or the total plan.

For a number of reasons, the offender's family may not have extended family or adequate resources to meet the obligations that a Family Group Conference requires. An example of this was a refugee family that had no extended family within New Zealand; the victim of the assault was one of the offender's caregivers. An arrangement was made with two migrant and refugee organizations to support the family.

When you visit the family in their home before the FGC, offer to put them in contact with one or more organizations that may be able to help them. This would include the opportunity for them to meet with the organization's representatives before the family decides whether or not to involve them in the FGC.

For a very serious charge, the plan may require high levels of supervision; spreading the burden can make the difference between success and failure. A failure may not be the fault of the young person, but rather the adult's lack of endurance in carrying out the supervision. Having other organizations and networks involved along with the family can make a great difference in the plan's succeeding.

Once the FGC is arranged, invitation letters should be sent out to all identified participants.

The Conference

Again, Family Group Conferences can take many forms, depending on the culture and/or religion of the participants. What is outlined in this section should only be used as a guide.

Steps through a Family Group Conference

1. Opening
- prayer, if appropriate
- introductions
- presentation of overview

2. Information sharing
- summary of facts
- review of victim impact
- offender response

- information about forming the plan
- refreshments (optional)

3. Family deliberations

4. Reaching agreement
- proposal
- negotiation
- finalization of plan

5. Closing
- prayer, if appropriate

Setting up the meeting room

Make sure that the room has adequate resources for the Conference. Space and seating are the most critical. Try to allow for more seating and space than may be required. This allows for more flexibility of choice by the participants.

Sometimes victims and their supporters might like to leave a seat or two between themselves and the offender's family. There will also be times when the offender's family feels uncomfortable sitting together; family dynamics may cause them to want space between them (e.g., the parents may be separated).

The seating arrangement may change during the course of the FGC as participants' comfort levels increase. For example, the offender may feel uncomfortable being with his/her family at the beginning of the FGC but may choose to sit with them by the conclusion of the FGC.

It is very important that the venue is free of interruption from unexpected visitors and phone calls. This can be a problem particularly if it is decided that the FGC will be held at a family's home. When this option is chosen, contract with the family to unplug the phone.

Other resources that are required include access to another room to facilitate private deliberations, and having pens and writing material in both rooms. It is also important to provide culturally-appropriate refreshments. Some participants may want to bring their own food to contribute since sharing food with the others may be an important part of their culture.

When laying out the seating, remember that a circle or horseshoe shape is often most appropriate, both culturally and to enhance communication. Discourage participants from sitting outside the circle. The seating arrangement should allow people to leave the room with a minimum of inconvenience and without having to walk past a person with whom they are in conflict.

Phase 1. Opening the Conference

As participants arrive, ask them to sit where they feel comfortable, but within the seating set up for the FGC.

If the family has indicated that they would like the FGC to start with a *blessing or prayer,* begin with that, offered by a member of the family or a support person. Often in New Zealand the blessing or prayer is said in the family's first language and in a way that is appropriate to their religion or culture. This is very important because it demonstrates your respect for the family's values. A member of the family can translate if the prayer is not in a language understood by all. On rare occasions the Coordinator may be asked to say a blessing or prayer on behalf of the FGC.

The next step is to start the *introductions;* this is the first step if there is no blessing or prayer. Lead the introductions by introducing yourself by your name and your official position. State that it is the Coordinator's responsibility to facilitate the Family Group Conference and to explain the process for the FGC after the introductions. Then ask the other participants to introduce themselves, starting from the Coordinator's left. (Many, but not all, cultures follow a clockwise direction in meetings that are set in a circle or horseshoe.)

Ask the participants to include in their introductions the reasons that they are there. Getting participants to introduce themselves helps start their involvement in the process better than if you introduce them to one another.

Once the introductions have been completed, *outline the legal standing of the FGC and the process* for *this particular FGC*. Remind the participants that there is flexibility, and that if they need private time or a break they only need to indicate to the Coordinator that they would like that opportunity. Also, make it very clear that it is the Coordinator's responsibility to make sure the principles that guide the Youth Justice process are not compromised in the FGC or through the agreed outcomes. After explaining the principles and process, ask if there are any questions.

It is important to give the participants good information on what they are about to undertake, but most of this should have been given to the key participants prior to the FGC. An overview at the start of the Family Group Conference should last only about five minutes.

Phase 2. Information sharing

Now the focus shifts to the offending behavior or act. In most cases this would start with the *reading of the summary* of facts by the police. This summary sets out the facts on which the charges, or intended charges, are based. If the charges are denied, the FGC can go no further because the matter needs to be forwarded or returned to court for a defended hearing. Family Group Conferences can only make decisions or recommendations on charges that are admitted or proven by the court. But if the young person is going to deny the charges, you would normally know this before you set up a Conference.

Next, ask the young person whether s/he understands the charges and what they mean; then ask whether s/he admits or denies the offense. Make it clear to the alleged offender before the FGC and during the explanation of the process that s/he should not admit any charge s/he is not sure s/he has committed.

After the child or young person has admitted the charge, ask the victim or victims *to explain the impact* the offenses have had on them. From the pre-Conference communication with the victim, the Coordinator will have an idea about what questions need to be asked to help bring out his/her story. Advise the victim that it is important for the young person to see his/her anger and hurt, if that is what s/he feels.

Often FGCs deal with a number of charges, which means that there could be more than one victim present, or that some victims may have chosen to attend while others have not. In this situation, the Coordinator needs to decide whether the information from the victims who have not attended should be stated at this time, or whether it is better to have the attending victims go first. Try to read the body language of the victims. If they are looking comfortable or give an impression that they want to have their say, always have them go first. If they are looking hesitant or unlikely to share their feelings, then offer the absent victims' information first, trying to project into the FGC their anger and hurt, so the victims present feel more comfortable sharing theirs.

After the victims have shared their stories, you may wish to summarize the impact. Then ask the child or young person to tell the victims why s/he committed the offenses. If necessary, help the young person share his/her information. When the young person is done, it may be helpful to summarize what s/he has said. You may also want to ask the offender how s/he feels about what s/he has heard, and perhaps even whether s/he has anything to say to the victim. However, you may also wish to wait and see what emerges from the family caucus.

This can be the point where the victims start asking *questions* of the child or young person. If this leads to a natural flowing communication between the victim and the offender, it is important for the Coordinator to reduce his or her facilitation.

The first objective when facilitating a FGC is to establish communication between the two parties. When that communication comes to a natural end, you may want to ask the offender's family to summarize how the offense has impacted them. Also ask the family to tell the FGC what they would like the FGC to hear about their child/young person's actions, any other statements they may wish to make, or questions they may wish to ask. It is critical to develop the communication between the victims and the offending young person and his/her family.

Youth advocates who attend FGCs know that their job is not adversarial and that they are there to be supportive, providing information or advice, but not interfering with the process. Before the offender's family moves into its private deliberation, you may wish to ask such professionals whether they have any further information they would like to give the offender's family.

Phase 3. Family caucus and deliberations

Once all the relevant information has been shared, prepare for family deliberations. The offender's family is entitled to have private deliberations and the Coordinator must offer it to them, although they may choose not to take it. Before this happens, though, it may help to summarize the harms and impacts, as well as the preventive issues, that the offender's family will need to address. It is important to provide the family with newsprint and markers to use in planning or presenting.

This is a time when most FGCs take a break for refreshments. Family deliberations often come more naturally when they follow or include refreshments.

As the Coordinator, be sure to observe what happens at this point. If the participants stay together, the healing has already started. If the victim and his/her support have prepared their refreshments and moved into the other room, it may indicate that they are still feeling uncomfortable. The most common reason for a victim to feel uncomfortable generally comes from a perceived lack of remorse from the offender.

It is wise to engage the victim in conversation by asking him/her how s/he feels about the FGC to this point. When there is a perceived lack of remorse, it is important to advise the victim that an offending child or young person is often unable to show his/her remorse until after the deliberations with his/her family, and explain why. The young person often enters the process with his/her own defense mechanisms well engaged, but after hearing the impact s/he has had on the victim and seeing the anger, and then talking with his/her own family, s/he is better able to let down his/her defenses.

The offender's family should be made aware that, if they wish, they can invite any of the FGC participants to come in to their deliberations to answer questions. This often occurs. Sometimes the family just wants to check that they are moving towards a plan that is going to be acceptable to the victim before they invest more time in it.

The family caucus provides an opportunity for:
- the offender and his/her family to discuss family matters and begin developing a plan;
- the victim and his/her supporters to talk about their needs and options with the coordinator, police, and other participants.

These family deliberations are a very critical part of the process for a number of reasons. First, the offender and his/her family have a chance to talk in private about the options and resources they have within the family. They may have been reluctant to put another family member on the spot in the larger forum. In private, they are able to investigate more personal issues like financial commitments, or personal requests for support from the extended family to cover resource needs, including time commitments that may be required to supervise parts of the plan.

Frequently, a family has to deal with issues within the family before they can focus on establishing a plan to address the offense. If the parents have separated, the incident can highlight the need for them to make new commitments about parenting or to decide with whom the young person will reside while s/he is held account-able for the offense. During the deliberations, the family may request that the Coordinator or another Conference participant join them for a short time to answer questions.

Victims often use this time to reflect with the police about what they would like to see in the plan and why. This is very positive, since the police feel more comfortable agreeing to a plan that meets the victims' needs. During this time, too, the victims are able to talk with their own support people and other Conference participants.

When the offender's family returns from their private deliberations, there is often a change of seating arrange-ments. For example, the youth may now sit with his or her family instead of sitting separately.

Phase 4. Reaching agreement

Offenders' families bring back quite varied suggestions. They may present a comprehensive plan, or a list of beginning ideas, or simply a statement that they have addressed only personal issues and now wish to put the plan together in the larger group. It is important not to make an initial judgment about what is presented at this point. Most often the family has an outline of a plan, but they want the larger group to assist them with the finer details.

Encourage the offending child/young person to present the plan. There are two main reasons for this. If the child/young person can present the plan, then the Coordinator can be reasonably comfortable that s/he understands it. Also, this tends to put the focus of the conversation back between the offender and the victim or victims.

After the young person has presented the plan that s/he and his/her family have developed, without interruption ask the victim what s/he would like to add or remove from the plan. Do this in a way that empowers the victim to feel s/he has a right to contribute to the plan. Avoid asking yes/no questions; don't ask the victim if s/he agrees or disagrees with the plan but encourage discussion on the plan with open-ended questions.

Once the victim has expressed his/her wishes and worked out the details with the offending young person and his/her family, it is time to involve the professionals (police and Youth Advocate). It is rare for the police representative to want an amendment that will take a victim's wish out of the plan, or something that has been offered to the victim. Rather, the police tend to focus on the public interest. When they know the victim's interests, the police are in a better position to weigh those alongside the community's interests.

The next step is not to ask for agreement on the plan, but to take more time to explore how the offender's family perceives the plan. Often a family member may express a wish that s/he is not sure how to implement. It is very important that the Coordinator does not make the decision, but offers a number of options from which the victim, as well as the offending young person and family, can choose. For example, a victim may say s/he would like to be kept informed of how the child/young person is progressing with the plan, but the young person is not sure how to meet this desire. The Coordinator can suggest that they consider a number of options with varying levels of interaction, ranging from a letter to the victim from the young person near the end of the plan, to reconvening the FGC to review progress.

Some joint activity to celebrate the successful completion of the plan is a way of bringing positive closure to a challenging situation for all involved. The offending young person's family may invite the victim to their home for a celebratory barbecue or meal. Such ideas provide additional motivation for the young person to complete the plan.

Once the plan is outlined, it is important to have a *reality check*. Go through the plan and make sure that

---

Core elements in a plan

- Putting things right for the victim (a priority).

- Returning something to the community.

- Addressing the underlying causes of the offending.

- Ensuring that the child/young person has the support s/he needs to meet his/her obligations.

---

each of the decisions is measurable and able to be monitored. Each decision needs to include a date by when it should be completed, who will insure that it is carried out, and what and how much needs to be undertaken. A community-work decision could read as follows:

Community Work

Robert will complete 40 hours of community work, with a minimum of five hours being completed per week. Robert's mother will arrange for this work to start within two weeks at the Salvation Army's home for the elderly. Verification will be through a letter from the Salvation Army recording the hours completed, which will be forwarded to the monitor of the plan.

Once all the outcomes have been made clear and measurable, ask the victim if s/he agrees with the total plan as presented. Then ask the offending young person's family if they agree; then seek the agreement of the police. If the victim is not present, let the participants know that you will contact the victim the next day to confirm that it meets with his/her needs or wishes.

It is important to ask the offending young person, "Do you believe you can complete this plan?" Explore any hesitancies with him/her. Even if s/he says yes, ask whether s/he feels that s/he is being set up to fail in any way. The aim is to ensure that the young person is not just saying yes to avoid the pressure of the moment. If his/her concern is opened up, more assistance can be provided to get him/her through the parts s/he views as being difficult. If the fear is about being home alone or having to keep a curfew, see if s/he could spend that time with another family member or a supportive friend.

When there is full agreement to the plan (which occurs in over 95% of FGCs), advise the offending young person to let the police, or social worker, or community representative, know if something beyond his/her control is preventing him/her from completing the plan.

When participants in a Conference cannot agree, there are two ways in which that outcome can be recorded. But first, let us state clearly that the negotiations within a Conference should be recorded "without prejudice." Therefore, if there is no agreement to any plan at all, the facilitator of the Conference should record only that the Conference could not reach agreement. Do not record the views of the different parties.

The plan in 4 parts

1. System issues

2. Reparation

3. Prevention

4. Monitoring

If, however, the participants do reach agreement on most parts of the plan, they could agree to record the points on which they have agreement. Without noting the views or positions of the parties, the facilitator could record that agreement couldn't be reached on a specific point. For example, "The Conference was unable to make a recommendation on how the matter should be disposed, once the plan is completed," or "The Conference agreed that community work should be done but could not agree on the amount." This makes it clear to the court where some arbitration may be required.

Phase 5. Closing the Conference

If the meeting started with a blessing/prayer, then it usually should be closed with a blessing/prayer.

It is not uncommon for participants to remain and talk for a few minutes after the FGC has concluded, which clearly reflects the process's ability to bring people together who were separated by conflict. In many cases, victims offer offenders employment so they can pay off the reparation, but at a rate that still leaves the offender with money (e.g. a 50/50 split of his/her earnings until the reparation is paid in full).

In some cases, victims have had the offender socialize with them so the offender can find a new peer group or come to their home to make repairs. There is no limit on what can be put in a Family Group Conference plan under New Zealand law, with two exceptions: the maximum number of community work hours that can be ordered is 200, and court-ordered reparation is limited to actual loss and not to consequential or secondary loss.

The plan

The format of the plan is important. The best format is one that is clear and that groups the outcomes into the areas to which they apply. *All parts of the plan, including*

Case example

In one Family Group Conference I facilitated, six organizations were represented. For the plan to succeed, they needed to work cooperatively together and ensure that the commitments they made in the Conference would be completed.

The plan was completed successfully and a letter was sent out to inform all the participants. Shortly thereafter, I received a call from the victim. He told me he left the Conference feeling it wouldn't work. He felt the process was good, but went on to tell me that he had been a public servant his entire working career. He said the last thing a government department did was work cooperatively with another department or community organization, and it was this experience that led him to believe the plan would fail.

The plan relied on four government departments and two community organizations working cooperatively together. He was impressed that the conferencing process had the strength to overcome these long-established barriers.

---

deadlines and expectations, should be spelled out clearly.
The following is a recommended four-part format.

Part 1: System issues

Specify what the Conference is requesting of the agency having jurisdiction, e.g., police, prosecutor, or court. For instance, the outcomes may state that the police or the prosecutor have agreed not to take any further action if the plan is successfully completed, or that the Conference is recommending that charges be taken before the court. If the case is, or is to be, before the court, the plan could recommend how the matter is to be monitored by the court. It could state that the Conference requests that the court adjourn the matter until the agreed-upon plan is completed, and if the plan is successfully completed, the matters could be withdrawn or discharged without any formal record. Alternatively, if the case has been referred from court, the Conference could recommend the overall sentence in which they would like to see the plan included.

Part 2: Reparation

This part should record the outcomes which focus on the offender "putting right" for the victim and community. These are outcomes such as reparation, restitution, and community work. This allows the victim to see clearly what is being done for him/her and keeps the Conference focused on its main purpose.

Part 3: Prevention

This part contains the outcomes that address the underlying causes for the offending and are aimed at assisting the offender to keep his/her promises to the victim. As examples, outcomes here could include drug and alcohol counseling, family counseling, or supervision contracts.

Part 4: Monitoring

The monitoring of the Family Group Conference plan is as important as any other part of the FGC process. Adults and/or organizations giving support to the plan must have the tenacity to see the plan through to its conclusion. In most cases where a plan fails, it is the supervising adults who fail to carry through.

The plan should specify just who is monitoring what, to whom they are to report, and what deadlines exist for each part of the plan. The best way to achieve good monitoring is to share the responsibility and write particular assignments into each individual outcome. In the final section of the plan, record to whom each monitoring person will report as each part is completed. It is a good practice to record how often the monitoring person(s) will make contact with the young person to check progress.

Let us repeat, monitoring is greatly assisted if the outcomes are measurable. Be sure to specify who, when, where, and how much. Recording when a particular outcome will start and the date it is due to be completed will greatly enable the monitoring process.

Avoid outcomes that say "reasonable" (reasonable to whom?) and have other unclear requirements, in order to escape debates about whether the spirit of the plan was completed or not.

Put as much responsibility as possible on the offending young person and his/her family. Remember that one of the principles is to foster the ability of the family to develop its own means of dealing with a child or young person of theirs who offends.

Note that when the youth has successfully completed the plan, all the participants are to be notified. If a closing meeting or celebration is included in the plan, this should now be arranged.

Extending the family

The FGC process has worked best when it has drawn upon the extended family and/or community support for the offender's family. Following are some suggestions about how to help this to happen.

The *extended family* should always be the first resource to be considered. However, some extended families are unable to be the resource that is required. This may be due to a number of reasons, including age, distance, illness, or the fact that they have their hands full with other members of the family. For a variety of causes, then, families may need help beyond their own resources, and this is one area where the process may need to be enhanced. Otherwise, one or both of the following two situations is likely to occur.

The first is that the process will require the family to open up its baggage for all to see, resulting in shame that will prove destructive and add to the family's sense of failure. The most likely outcome of this will be that the young person and his/her family will make commitments and promises that they feel obligated to make but will never be able to fulfill. The process could set them up to fail without benefiting anyone.

The second possibility is that the Conference will make concessions so that the outcomes are achievable. But the victim will bear most of the cost of these less productive outcomes. A family that can barely meet their day-to-day living costs may be able to agree to only minimal reparation. Compare that to an outcome in one case where the family not only met the reparation cost, but also gave each of the two victims a gift of a thousand dollars within four weeks. The extended family and their community raised the money through running sausage sizzles, car washes, and a stall at the local market. The young person in turn was committed to assist that group to fundraise for the next year. The network of support made it possible for this offender and his family to fully meet, and even go beyond, their obligation to the victim.

Restorative justice is a community-building process.

For these reasons, it is important to have a network of support available for offenders' families. The network needs to have variety and choice for the family. This network can be used to spread the burden in all aspects of the process for the family. Community groups can provide a number of resources to assist in the implementation and monitoring of the plan. Often they have services and programs that can be offered to the family, and, because they have the potential to be culturally appropriate, they can also provide helpful role models for the offender and his/her family.

4.

Beyond the Family Group Conference

My (Allan's) experience in Wellington and elsewhere has demonstrated that Family Group Conferences are most effective as part of a community-wide effort. This requires that community groups and organizations not only be drawn into the Conferences and their follow-up, but that they also be made part of an effort to address the patterns of youth offending in general.

Involving community groups as part of the overall Conference process gives them an opportunity to work in a cooperative way that will enhance their effectiveness, avoid duplication of services, and enable them to provide a "no gaps" service to the offending young person and his/her family. Their understanding of the commitments the young person and his/her family are required to make often further enhances the organization's effectiveness.

Funding for community initiatives is often spread very lightly through the community. Experience shows that when community agencies work together in the FGC process, they establish relationships that enable them to continue working together and to use their resources more effectively.

Conferencing the Conferences

The effectiveness of these community groups can be increased by "conferencing the results of the Conferences." The Coordinators who are involved in these Conferences, along with the police, are often able to see patterns and trends in the communities which are leading to youth offending. By helping community groups to come together and address these patterns that contribute to crime, Coordinators can spearhead the development of prevention strategies.

In one Conference, the facilitator asked me to be support for the victim because he and his mother were alone. The son had been brutally beaten. Neither the victim nor his mother wanted to be at the Conference with the offender.

The offending youth's family, of mixed heritage, was at odds with each other. They argued continually among themselves in front of the Conference. During the victim's time to speak, the offending youth's mother felt her son was being verbally attacked. The facilitator made an appropriate statement to the youth's mother, and then calmed the group enough to continue.

But, after a very lengthy family alone time, there was a huge change. The offender's family had worked together and created a workable, just plan. The youth and his family also apologized sincerely for what had happened to the woman's son. I remember the relaxed, smiling face of the victim's mother as she spoke to the facilitator and me after the Conference, saying that she experienced justice and hope, and that now she and her son could put this ugly incident behind them.

— An anonymous observer

Community groups who address causes, combined with the close collaboration of the Youth Aid Officers (the "youth police") and the Youth Justice Coordinator, account for the dramatic results in reducing youth crime achieved in Wellington, the capital city of New Zealand, over a three-year period and beyond. In Wellington, we (Allan and others) were able to identify the common factors among a group of youth who were accounting for 58% of youth court appearances.

Among these was a tendency for young Maori offenders to be out of touch with their heritage and community. Because of what we had learned in FGCs, we were uniquely able to assist a Maori community-service organization to develop a proposal which addressed the factors that were contributing to their young people's offending. We were also able to provide information to potential funding agencies about why it was important to underwrite the initiative. The proposal was financed, and a six-month program was implemented. The results of the well-focused initiative were astounding: the offending group disappeared totally from our court statistics. The number of burglaries and car thefts in Wellington dropped dramatically within the six-month term of the program and has remained low.

Another example of "conferencing the Conferences" involved addressing peer group issues. Parents often find they are competing against peer influences, and so do the plans that come out of an FGC. I would often witness genuine remorse and commitment from the young person at the end of the Conference, but within weeks I would see that commitment being undermined by his/her peer group. I also noted that most of the peer group came through FGCs for offending in similar ways. I realized we did not need to wait for each youth to come through individually. Within three Conferences we would know who the peer group was. They were mainly identified on the non-association lists (lists of young people the family wants its child to avoid) the parents put forward because of the negative influence the parents believed they had on their child/young person.

Once I had sufficient information about the issues that were contributing to the youth offending within the community, I asked the appropriate community agencies to

---

A young 13- or 14-year-old girl of Samoan-White heritage, who lived on the streets, had attempted to steal a woman's purse. The FGC for this case had about 40 people in attendance. The girl was obviously distraught. She was hunched over and dazed, and the sadness from her body seemed to permeate the whole room. Her Samoan mother, with breast cancer, was in Australia. Her father, married sister, and adult family friends were present, along with social workers, the police, and others. Her "aunties" from the Samoan side of her family were there, as was her cultural community, including elders who could hardly move. Yet they were there to support her.

The FGC spent a very long time together during the family caucus. When we all reassembled to hear the plan they came up with, the group encouraged the girl to present it. Upon returning to the Conference circle, the girl physically looked like a different person. She was vibrant. She not only presented the plan well, she, and now everyone there, laughed and joked. The entire group showed genuine care for this beautiful child. It was a blessing to see.

—An anonymous observer

One evening I accompanied a facilitator to an evening meeting at a local cultural center. Before the meeting started, we ate and socialized. A young man came over and sat down beside me. He introduced himself. Through our conversation, I told him that I was there to study the FGC process. He said, "Oh, yeah, I've been to a few of those."

I said, "Really, could you tell me about them?"

He said casually, "They were FGCs for *me*."

Then he went on to praise the process and said that the FGCs turned him around. He said he did a lot of cultural work now, had a wonderful wife and baby, and a job he was proud of. I asked what he did. He said he was in the janitorial maintenance field. I said it sounded as if he'd found the right job. He said, "I absolutely have. I work at McDonald's, I do all the cleaning—tables, floors, toilets. I love it."

He made me feel that with that kind of sincerity and sense of self-worth, he'll probably own a few McDonald's before he's finished. Here he had run with the wolves, and now he's running with life.

— An anonymous observer

come together in a series of meetings.

The agencies I asked to meet included four or more community groups, the police, and education providers. I shared the profile I had on the offending group and facilitated the other participants in sharing their knowledge. The process of the meeting was nearly the same as many FGCs follow: information-sharing with the community groups, allowing them time to deliberate among themselves and prepare suggestions, and then the facilitated negotiation towards an agreement. At the end of the meeting we had an outline of a plan. I took this away and turned it into a draft proposal. I then reconvened the meeting after the participating groups had a chance to look at the draft proposal. From the second meeting, I obtained the information I needed to finalize the proposal and gain the groups' commitment to it.

The last step was to advocate for any extra resources that were required to put the proposals into an action plan. These were a lot easier to fund than the usual proposals, because at this point they already had government, agency, community, and police support.

Through this combined community-based strategy, we had marshalled support for the whole peer group to make changes. It was not long before the peer groups started supporting each other in positive ways and the negative influence disappeared from the Conference process. We had also created a program to which we can refer youth and their families.

In working this way, community groups have gained extra resources and experience, making them more effective for future Family Group Conferences. This is not just a short-term benefit, because their reputations are enhanced and funding agencies are more prepared to finance them. As Coordinator I am able to advocate better for them, because I can quote clear achievements that are supported by unmistakably positive statistics. The community groups have also gained a better understanding of what services are required and how they can be made user-friendly for youth. This has led to some major service delivery changes that have proven valuable in empowering families and have also made the community organizations excellent monitors of Conference plans.

Within a three-year period, Wellington experienced about a two-thirds drop in youth offending. In 1996, we addressed 554 charges. In 1999, we addressed 174. The number of Conferences required dropped over the same period from 160 to 78. We believe it was due to three main factors: effective Family Group Conferences, close working between the police and the Youth Justice Coordinator, and a collaborative, community-based initiative to address the causes of offending behavior.

Conferencing is not a soft option; it was introduced to New Zealand as tough justice. It has been highly successful.

A story

I (Allan) held a Conference for a young person who was a refugee. He had come to New Zealand with his grandmother, who was his caregiver, and an aunt. New Zealand had only just started taking refugees from this young man's country, so there were no other family members and, in fact, few other residents of his culture nearby. The three arrived in New Zealand with nothing but what they could carry. Their only income was from a benefit paid by the New Zealand government, which provided for only the very basics of food and accommodation.

The charge was serious; the young person had assaulted his grandmother for cash. He had taken the rent money, and the grandmother was afraid of what would happen now that she could not pay it. In desperation, she reported the incident to the aunt, who in turn reported it to the police.

The police referred the case to an FGC without making an arrest. I met with the grandmother and aunt to consult on what format the Conference might follow and, in particular, what cultural and/or religious process should guide it. In this meeting I learned that the grandmother had been assaulted on more than one occasion and that she did not know where to go for assistance.

I met with the young person to explain the process to him and to see if he could identify any possible supports. It was agreed that I would invite his teacher, but it was clear this was not going to be enough. I contacted two organizations: Victims as Survivors, and the Refugee and Migrants Services Trust. Neither organization had been involved with Family Group Conferencing but agreed to assist. I asked one to be the direct support for the grandmother and the other to help the young person meet his obligations to his grandmother.

I then arranged for the grandmother to meet with the supporting organization so that she could share her story with them. They, in turn, would help her share her story at the Conference. I advised the grandmother that they would also transport her to the Conference and see her safely back home. And I also arranged for the young person to meet with his supporting organization. They agreed that they would assist him in developing a plan to put things right and support him to complete it.

The Conference started with a prayer in their native language, and all parties used interpreters to ensure full understanding. The grandmother told her story in much detail, as did the young person. As the young person began to understand the impact he was having on his grandmother, tears came to his eyes. The young man eventually told of his life in a refugee camp before the three arrived in New Zealand, what he had to do to survive, and how in his new community he felt he could not mix with others if he did not have money. Clearly, loneliness, anger, and hurt were shared by both the young man and his grandmother.

The plan that came out of the Conference required the young person to pay in full all the money he had taken. He was given help to find part-time employment. It was agreed that he could not live with his grandmother until she felt safe with him in the house. The plan provided also for counseling to help him overcome the anger that he carried from his experiences in the refugee camp. A mentor was found from his own culture who would check that he kept his promises and put things right with his grandmother. The putting right called for him to cook a meal for his grandmother and to make an apology. He was also required to complete community work and attend school every day. He would receive support with his homework.

The plan was successful. The young man did no further offending, and he completed all his outcomes. Most valuable of all, both he and his grandmother found new friends and support that stayed with them, well beyond the Family Group Conference plan, and assisted them in starting their new lives in New Zealand.

In Closing

Since the publication of the *Little Book of Family Group Conferences*, New Zealand's model has inspired innovations in a number of countries. In the United States, one promising application is in California where family group conferences are being used to keep young people out of the system entirely. The approach is designed to help meet the needs of those who have been harmed while supporting the positive development of those who have caused harm. Another goal is to address racial disparities in the justice system by diverting young people of color from the "school to prison pipeline."

Adapted from the New Zealand model, the conferences (called Restorative Community Conferences) include the young person who caused the harm and family members, the person harmed and their supporters, community members, and occasionally law enforcement. By agreement with the prosecutor, facilitators are able to offer a "reverse Miranda"—that is, the process is confidential and information revealed will not be used against them in later proceedings. Dialogue in the conferences addresses the crime, its causes and effects, and a plan. These consensus-based plans have four parts: to "do right" by one's victim, family, community and self. When the plan is completed within 3–6 months, the case is closed without charges being filed.

The conferences have been found to be most effective with more serious crimes that have an identifiable victim such as robbery, burglary, car theft, assault and battery, arson, teen dating violence, and sexual assault. Recidivism rates have been remarkably low for those who complete the process; at the time of this publication, the rate was 11.8 percent. Ninety-nine percent of the Almeda County victims who participated in these conferences say they would participate in another.

For more information, see http://www.impactjustice.org.

Selected Readings

Books:

Hayden, Anne. *Restorative Conferencing Manual of Aotearoa New Zealand.* Dept. for Courts, New Zealand, 2001. (Orders may be placed through Anne Molloy, anne.molloy@courts.govt.nz.)

Brown, B.J. and F.W.M McElrea, eds. *The Youth Court in New Zealand: A New Model of Justice.* Legal Research Foundation, New Zealand, 1993. (Orders may be placed through Jane Kilgour at j.kilgour@auckland.ac.nz)

Galaway, Burt et. al., eds. *Family Group Conferences: Perspectives on Policy and Practice.* Criminal Justice Press, 1995.

Internet:

http://www.cyf.govt.nz/youth-justice/family-group-conferences.html

http://www.restorativejustice.org

https://www.iirp.edu/lib_online_collection.php

http://www.rj4all.info

Books on restorative justice:

Consedine, Jim. *Restorative Justice: Healing the Effects of Crime.* 2nd edition, Plowshares, New Zealand, 1999.

Johnstone, Gerry. *Restorative Justice: Ideas, Values, and Debates.* Willam Publishing, UK, 2002.

Zehr, Howard. *Changing Lenses: Restorative Justice for Our Times.* 25th anniversary edition, Herald Press, 2015.

Zehr, Howard. *The Little Book of Restorative Justice.* Good Books, 2002.

Acknowledgments

I wish to acknowledge those who assisted with the work reflected in this book. First, I must acknowledge the Maori people and, in particular, those involved with Kahungunu Ki Poneke Community Services and Mokai Kainga Maori Centre. Their guidance and support of young people have constantly inspired me.

I acknowledge the Wellington Youth Aid Service of the New Zealand Police for working in partnership with my position to develop the best practice model available throughout New Zealand. Their participation in Family Group Conferences and their commitment to the plans that came out of the process contributed greatly to the model's success.

I acknowledge Judge Henwood. She allowed and encouraged the working model to flourish in Wellington through partnership, coordination, and cooperation.

Lastly, I acknowledge KPMG Consulting who recognized and promoted the importance of the work in Wellington. They gave the model the National Supreme Award for Innovation that honored all who participated in its development.

— Allan MacRae

We also wish to thank the following for their suggestions on various drafts of the manuscript: Dee Tompkins, Carl Stauffer, Bonnie Price Lofton, Jarem Sawatsky, Rita Hatfield, Jessalyn Nash, and Judge FWM McElrea. In spite of all this feedback, however, we take full responsibility for the views and for any inaccuracies in this book.

— Allan MacRae and Howard Zehr

Appendices

Research and Statistics

In June 2003, New Zealand researcher Gabriel Maxwell released the results of a major research project following up 1003 young people in New Zealand who had FGCs in 1998, with additional data from other cases. The following summarizes some of the conclusions of this study:

- The number of cases going to Youth Court has dropped dramatically since the introduction of the 1989 Act, from 600 per 10,000 cases in Youth Court in 1987, to about 250 per 10,000 in 2001.

- Cases resulting in incarceration of young people have also dropped significantly, from about 300 in 1987 to well under 100 in 2001.

- Almost all FGCs (90%) contained measures to ensure young offenders' accountability, and in over 80% of the cases the required tasks were successfully completed. Eighty percent of the accountability plans included repair of harm that had been caused.

- About half of the plans included measures to enhance the well-being of the young person—rehabilitative and/or reintegrative.

- The process goals of ensuring that appropriate people—including victims and families—participate, and that a consensus process be used, appear to be largely achieved. Not all victims attended, but that was mainly because not all chose to do so.

- Since participating in an FGC, most of the young people were able to develop positive goals and achieve successes, although some did continue to have negative life experiences and to re-offend. Other research cited suggests that if more good quality programs were provided as follow-up to the conferences, outcomes would be even more positive.

- Over the years since the introduction of the 1989 Act, the youth justice system has continued to grow in strength and has become more restorative. As part of this, the police have developed their own diversionary practices that reflect restorative rather than punitive philosophies. Similarly, the Youth Court appears to have become more inclusive. Victims more often appear to feel positively than in the early years. Reintegrative and rehabilitative programs are being offered to young offenders as well.

  At the same time, there is considerable room for improvement in practice, e.g., in increasing participation and consensus, in addressing cultural issues, and in reducing reliance on Youth Court.

Much more research on FGCs is now available not only from New Zealand but other contexts where the model has been adapted. Some of this can be found by searching websites such as these: http://www.restorativejustice.org, https://www.iirp.edu/lib_online_collection.php and http://www.rj4all.info.

> *"The research demonstrates that the nature of the youth justice process does affect critical outcomes for young people: both in terms of reducing offending and increasing the possibility of other positive life outcomes. Restorative practices that include empowerment, the repair of harm, and reintegrative outcomes make a positive difference, while the extent of embeddedness in the criminal justice system, severe and retributive outcomes, and stigmatic shaming have negative effects."*
> — Gabriel Maxwell
> June, 2003

Benefits of Family Group Conferences

For victims

Victims who participate in FGCs have a chance to tell their offenders about the impact the offenses have on them. By meeting with offenders they gain a better understanding of what happened and why. They also have an opportunity to identify what they need in order for things to be put right. As is true of restorative justice programs elsewhere, a higher proportion of reparation is collected for victims when it is agreed to through a Conference rather than when it is simply court-ordered. Victims often find their offenders less intimidating after meeting with them, leading to an increased sense of safety. Often the victims are linked with support that they have not been aware of until informed of their rights as part of the Conference convening process. Overall, involvement in the FGC process contributes to a sense of empowerment for victims.

For the young person

In addition to having a better understanding of the impact of his/her behavior, the youth has the opportunity to earn back respect, to develop under the guidance of appropriate adult role models, and to maintain and develop the skills required for living successfully within a community. Opportunities can be provided for the youth to move into a more positive peer group and to be linked to his/her cultural community for support and guidance. Cultural supports have proven to be the most effective at getting the child/youth to complete his/her obligations to the victim.

For the offending youth's family

The family can be supported to be more effective, both with the child/youth that has offended and with other siblings. The family has the opportunity to remove the shame and sense of failure that comes through the offending committed by its family member. The family often gains long-term support networks. Isolated families can be linked to their residential and cultural communities.

For the community

The FGC process provides information that can empower the community to effectively address issues that contribute to offending within their community. FGCs promote closer and more effective relationships between government and community agencies. The process offers less costly responses. In New Zealand, millions have been saved in custody and court costs. The process provides the community with a greater opportunity to be involved, allows members of the community to be recognized as victims, and provides a way for the community to take appropriate responsibility for its members.

For the police

The FGC process empowers the police to seek appropriate outcomes. They gain substantially greater information about the community which they police, leading them to be better prepared to use their resources more effectively. FGCs help the police build a closer and more effective relationship with youth, their families, and their community, and to be better respected by those with whom they deal.

Sample Proposal to Address Peer Groups

Following is a basic outline of a proposal to address peer group issues. The proposal was developed to address the underlying causes of inappropriate behavior among a specific group of young people in Wellington. Not all had been charged with offending, but some had, and we strongly suspected that they all were involved in the same activities.

We expected to see these young people continue to be charged with further offending, but once this proposal was enacted, not one had another Conference, nor did any appear in court over the next three years while I was in Wellington. The project cost $14,000 New Zealand dollars. The proposal worked because it identified needs and matched up resources through an extended Conference process. *This was a program built around the needs of a specific group rather than forcing the group to fit within the needs of a program.*

A. Issues that were addressed in the proposal:
  a. Drug and/or alcohol abuse.
  b. Living outside the education system; truancy.
  c. Little or no networks in the community; not feeling part of their community or culture.
  d. No or inappropriate adult role models.
  e. Anger because of suffering some form of trauma, mainly through physical or mental abuse.

B. The plan for the Maori youth included:
  1. Group work on drug and alcohol abuse.
  2. Learning Maori songs and traditional dances.
  3. Learning a life skills program, including moving towards independence.
  4. Activities that put them in contact with support people in their immediate communities and their culture.
  5. Anger management.
  6. Driving lessons provided by the police.
  7. First Aid course funded by the police.
  8. Support, assistance, and education for parents.

C. The proposal had the following goals:
  1. All youth would be in formal education or be employed at the end of six months.
  2. The group would participate in the Ratana Church celebrations that would be held in the full Maori tradition. This goal required many hours of team training and practice.
  3. The youth would complete a three-day canoe trip to celebrate their achievement of the above goals.

Types of FGCs in New Zealand

There are four types of FGCs for youth offenders.

- *Intention to Charge Conference.* In this Conference, the police have decided they are prepared to charge the young person, but the youth is not under arrest. The Conference explores the resources available to it and whether the matter can be addressed without going to court. If it is agreed that the matter should go to court, the Conference will make a recommendation that the enforcement agency should prosecute (lay the charges in court). If the Conference cannot reach agreement, the enforcement agency is free to proceed to court with the matter.

- *Custody Conference.* This Conference is automatically held when the court places a young person who has denied an offense in custody. This Conference is held to explore other options besides custody. If it is agreed that the young person should stay in custody, the FGC decides what sort of programs should occur for that young person while s/he is in custody. This Conference helps ensure that families have say over what happens for the young person.

- *Charge Not Denied Conference.* When a young person appears in court s/he is asked if s/he takes some responsibility for what occurred. This is usually done through the youth's advocate, a court-appointed lawyer, who indicates that the charge is not denied. This is not a formal plea of guilty. In these cases the court must direct an FGC to recommend how the charges could be handled. The Conference could agree to a recommendation that the charges be withdrawn from court, have a young person complete a plan while on remand, with or without bail conditions, and/or discharge the charges as if they were never laid in court. Alternatively, the FGC can recommend to the court what orders it should make and the plans for those orders. This Conference could also recommend that charges be amended to more accurately reflect the incident. On very serious charges, the Conference also recommends in what jurisdiction the case should be handled—Youth Court or District (adult) Court.

- *Charge Proven Conference.* The court calls for this Conference after a defended court hearing has found the young person guilty. In New Zealand, a Conference must be held before a court makes orders or sentences a young person. This applies to all charges other than murder or manslaughter. The Conference is convened to make recommendations to the court on the sentence or alternative outcomes.

About the Authors

Allan MacRae is Manager of Coordinators for the Southern Region of New Zealand, overseeing Family Group Conferences for both Youth Justice, and Care and Protection. Prior to taking this position, he was Youth Justice Coordinator for the capital city of Wellington.

After receiving the National Supreme Award for Innovation, Allan developed a program in Wellington which emerged as a leading model of Youth Justice. Subsequently, he was a lead trainer in the "Best Practice Road Show," designed to bring these practices to other areas of New Zealand. He also conducted numerous trainings in Belgium, Thailand, and the United States.

Allan received his diploma in Social Work from Victoria University and has 23 years of experience working with young offenders and at-risk youth.

Howard Zehr is considered a founder of the field of restorative justice. He lectures, trains, and consults internationally, including in New Zealand. His book *Changing Lenses: A New Focus for Crime and Justice* is considered a classic in the field.

Other publications include *Doing Life: Reflections of Men and Women Serving Life Sentences*; *Transcending: Reflections of Crime Victims*; and *The Little Book of Restorative Justice*. He is Co-Director of the graduate Center for Justice and Peacebuilding at Eastern Mennonite University (Harrisonburg, Virginia).

In 2003 he received the Annual PeaceBuilder Award from the New York Dispute Resolution Association and the Restorative Justice Prize from Prison Fellowship International "for significant contributions to the advancement of Restorative Justice around the world."

Howard received his B.A. from Morehouse College and his Ph.D. from Rutgers University.

THE LITTLE BOOK OF
Circle Processes

A New/Old Approach to Peacemaking

KAY PRANIS

Table of Contents

Introduction

"We're all lovers and we're all destroyers. We're all fright-
ened and at the same time we all want terribly to trust. This
is part of our struggle. We have to help what is most beauti-
ful to emerge in us and to divert the powers of darkness and
violence. I learn to be able to say, 'This is my fragility. I must
learn about it and use it in a constructive way.'"

— Jean Vanier[1]

Old things made new

Our ancestors gathered around a fire in a circle. Families
gather around the kitchen table in a circle. Now, we
are learning to gather in a circle as a community to solve
problems, support one another, and connect to one another.

A new way of bringing people together to understand
one another, strengthen bonds, and solve community
problems is blossoming in modern Western communities.
But this new way is really very old. It draws on the ancient Native American tradition of using a talking piece, an
object passed from person to person in a group and which
grants the holder sole permission to speak. It combines this
ancient tradition with contemporary concepts of democracy and inclusivity in a complex, multicultural society.

Peacemaking Circles are being used in a variety of
contexts. In neighborhoods they provide support for those
harmed by crime and help decide sentences for those who

commit crime. In schools, they create a positive classroom climate and resolve behavior problems. In the workplace, they help address conflict, and in social services they develop more organic support systems for people struggling to get their lives together.

Circles are being used in:

- neighborhoods
- schools
- workplaces
- social services
- justice systems

The Circle Process is a storytelling process. Every person has a story, and every story has a lesson to offer. In the Circle, people touch one another's lives by sharing stories that have meaning to them. As the following three vignettes suggest, stories unite people in their common humanity and help them appreciate the depth and beauty of the human experience.

• • •

A breathless first-grader runs up to the school administrator supervising the playground. "Mrs. Ticiu! Mrs. Ticiu!" he exclaims. "I need a talking piece!" Mrs. Ticiu reaches into her pocket, extracts a small plastic dinosaur, and offers it to the child. He grasps the dinosaur tightly in his fist and dashes off to join several other students who, moments earlier, were arguing. With the help of the talking piece, they discuss their disagreement and find a solution they all like.

• • •

Legislators, state policy analysts, state agency administrators, and youth workers sit at tables with adolescents who have gotten into trouble to discuss the state vision for delinquent youth in Minnesota. As a talking piece is passed around the table, each person gets an equal chance to hear and share perspectives. Everyone listens intently to each speaker. After thoughtful listening and discussion, each table reaches a consensus position regarding its assigned topic.

• • •

In an inner-city neighborhood, an adolescent and his mom sit in a Circle with nearly a dozen community members and justice system professionals, including a prosecutor and a public defender. The assembled group stands and joins hands to express gratitude for the opportunity to come together as a community to support this adolescent and his family. A talking piece is passed and introductions are made. Each welcomes the youth and his mother to the Circle.

As the talking pieces makes its second round, Circle participants ask the youth about his progress in school, his behavior at home, and his interests. Two members of the Circle have visited his school and offer to help him catch up with his schoolwork. The youth's mother expresses grave concern that he is leaving the house without her permission. She talks about her fears for him when he is out on the street after dark.

As the talking piece circulates among those present, Circle participants share fears and anxieties from their own adolescence. In dialogue with the youth, they express care and concern but also clear expectations about school attendance, homework, and checking in with Mom before leaving the house.

Both the youth and his mother respond warmly to the overtures of support and concern from the Circle. Both are able to listen to one another better with the use of the talking piece, and they leave with a better understanding of each other's concerns and frustrations.

The youth promises to comply with the agreement, and the group schedules another Circle meeting to check on his progress. The group stands and joins hands for a closing acknowledgment of the hard work done.

Peacemaking Circles like those described above are bringing people together as equals to have honest exchanges about difficult issues and painful experiences in an atmosphere of respect and concern for everyone. In increasingly varied settings, Peacemaking Circles are providing a space in which people from widely divergent perspectives can come together to speak candidly about conflict, pain, and anger and leave those conversations feeling good about themselves and about others.

The philosphy of Circles acknowledges that we are all in need of help and that helping others helps us at the same time.

The underlying philosophy of Circles acknowledges that we are all in need of help and that helping others helps us at the same time. The participants of the Circle benefit from the collective wisdom of everyone in the Circle. Participants are not divided into givers and receivers: everyone is both a giver and a receiver. Circles draw on the life experience and wisdom of all participants to generate new understandings of the problem and new possibilities for solutions.

Peacemaking Circles bring together the ancient wisdom of community and the contemporary value of respect for individual gifts, needs, and differences in a process that:

- honors the presence and dignity of every participant
- values the contributions of every participant

- emphasizes the connectedness of all things
- supports emotional and spiritual expression
- gives equal voice to all

About this book

This book is an overview of Peacemaking Circles and is designed to familiarize readers with the general nature of the process, its underlying philosophy, and ways the Peacemaking Circle Process can be used. It is not a detailed description of the process nor does it explain how to conduct Circles in general.

The book will explain how to conduct a simple Talking Circle, but this is not adequate preparation for leading more complex Circles. Facilitating a Circle requires more than putting chairs in a circle. Training in Circle facilitation is recommended before attempting to conduct a Circle in circumstances involving conflict, strong emotions, or victimization.[2]

Historical context

Peacemaking Circles draw directly from the tradition of the Talking Circle, common among indigenous people of North America. Gathering in a Circle to discuss important community issues was likely a part of the tribal roots of most people. Such processes still exist among indigenous people around the world, and we are deeply indebted to those who have kept these practices alive as a source of wisdom and inspiration for modern Western cultures.

In contemporary society and largely outside the scope of mainstream awareness, Circles have been used by small groups of non-indigenous people for over 30 years. Women's groups in particular have made extensive use of a formal Circle Process. Those Circles have primarily occurred in the contexts of individuals sharing their personal journeys in a supportive community. Some individuals have taken their experience with personal Circles into public settings, but a systemic effort to use Circles in mainstream public processes, such as criminal justice, is relatively new and grows out of work undertaken in Yukon, Canada, in the early 1990s.

An overview of Circles

A Peacemaking Circle is a way of bringing people together in which:

- everyone is respected
- everyone gets a chance to talk without interruption
- participants explain themselves by telling their stories
- everyone is equal—no person is more important than anyone else
- spiritual and emotional aspects of individual experience are welcomed

Peacemaking Circles are useful when two or more people:

- need to make decisions together
- have a disagreement
- need to address an experience that resulted in harm to someone
- want to work together as a team
- wish to celebrate
- wish to share difficulties
- want to learn from each other

The Peacemaking Circle is a container strong enough to hold:

- anger
- frustration
- joy
- pain
- truth
- conflict
- diverse world views
- intense feelings
- silence
- paradox

This book is about Circle work that originated in public settings—Circles used more in a context of community-building than in a context of personal development, though all effective Circles ultimately engage people on a personal level, connect people in deep and personal places, and therefore contribute to personal development. In the United States, Peacemaking Circles were introduced under the philosophy of restorative justice, which promotes including all those impacted by a crime in a process of understanding the harm of crime and devising strategies for repairing the harm.[3]

The Peacemaking Circle Process in the United States began in the Minnesota criminal justice system. Peacemaking Circles offered a way to include those harmed by crime, those who commit crime, and the community in a partnership with the justice system to determine the most effective response to a crime that would promote healing and safety for everyone. The goals of the Circle include developing support for those harmed by crime, deciding the sentence for those who commit crime and supporting them in fulfilling the obligations of the sentence, and strengthening the community to prevent crimes.

Rural, suburban, and urban communities are using the process for criminal cases involving both adult and juvenile crimes. Peacemaking Circles are active across a range of cultural communities including African American, Euro-American, Hmong, Latino, Cambodian, and Native American.

Though Circles began in the context of the sentencing process, corrections practitioners found other applications for this approach within the criminal justice system. Innovative professionals began using Circles to facilitate community re-entry for people who have been incarcerated and to improve the effectiveness of community supervision for people on probation.

> Circle Processes are part of the roots of most traditions.

Circles in Minnesota began as a part of the criminal justice process but soon found use elsewhere. Community volunteers working in Justice Circle projects quickly recognized that the process would be helpful in many situations not related to crime, so they took Circles into schools, workplaces, social services, churches, neighborhood groups, and their families.

The spread of Peacemaking Circles has been spontaneous and organic, seeds carried from one place to another by passion and commitment more than by strategic planning or organized dissemination.

1.
Circles in Practice

"I'm impressed with the gentleness of the Circle.
It arrives at something in such a gentle way."
— Circle participant in an alternative school

How does a Peacemaking Circle work?

Peacemaking Circles use structure to create possibilities for freedom: freedom to speak our truth, freedom to drop masks and protections, freedom to be present as a whole human being, freedom to reveal our deepest longings, freedom to acknowledge mistakes and fears, freedom to act in accord with our core values.

Participants sit in a circle of chairs with no tables. Sometimes objects that have meaning to the group are placed in the center as a focal point to remind participants of shared values and common ground. The physical format of the Circle symbolizes shared leadership, equality, connection, and inclusion. It also promotes focus, accountability, and participation from all.

Using very intentional structural elements—ceremony, a talking piece, a facilitator or keeper, guidelines, and consensus decision-making—Circles aim to create a space in which participants are safe to be their most authentic self. (These elements, explained briefly here, are addressed more fully in Chapter 6.)

Ceremony—Circles consciously engage all aspects of human experience—spiritual, emotional, physical, and mental. Circles use a ceremony or intentional centering activity in the opening and in the closing to mark the Circle as a sacred space in which participants are present with themselves and one another in a way that is different from an ordinary meeting.

A Talking Piece—By allowing only the person holding the talking piece to speak, a Circle regulates the dialogue as the piece circulates consecutively from person to person around the group. The person holding the talking piece has the undivided attention of everyone else in the Circle and can speak without interruption. The use of the talking piece allows for full expression of emotions, deeper listening, thoughtful reflection, and an unhurried pace. Additionally, the talking piece creates space for people who find it difficult to speak in a group, but it never requires the holder to speak.

A Facilitator or Keeper—The facilitator of the Peacemaking Circle, often called a keeper, assists the group in creating and maintaining a collective space in which each participant feels safe to speak honestly and openly without disrespecting anyone else. The keeper monitors the quality of the collective space and stimulates the reflections of the group through questions or topic suggestions. The keeper does not control the issues raised by the group or try to move the group toward a particular outcome, but the keeper may take steps to address the tone of the group interaction.

Guidelines—Participants in a Circle play a major role in designing their own space by creating the guidelines for their discussion. The guidelines articulate the promises participants make to one another about how they will conduct themselves in the Circle dialogue. The guidelines are intended to describe the behaviors that the participants feel will make the space safe for them to speak their truth. Guidelines are not rules and they are not used to judge people's behavior. They are used as gentle reminders to participants about their shared commitment to creating a safe space for difficult conversation.

Consensus Decision-Making—Decisions in a Circle are made by consensus. Consensus does not require enthusiasm for the decision or plan, but it does require that each participant is willing to live with the decision and support its implementation.

In a Circle, relationship-building and getting to know one another beyond the context of the task precede discussion about the task itself. Half the time of a Circle may be spent on creating the foundation for deeply honest dialogue about the conflict or difficulty before that dialogue begins. Discussing values, creating guidelines, and sharing unseen aspects of ourselves are all part of creating the foundation for dialogue that engages participants' spirits and emotions as well as their intellect.

> Wisdom
> in a Circle
> is accessed
> through
> personal
> stories.

Wisdom in a Circle is accessed through personal stories. In a Circle, life experience is more valuable than advice. Participants share their experiences of joy and pain, struggle and triumph, vulnerability and strength to understand the issue at hand. Because storytelling engages people on many levels—emotional, spiritual, physical, and mental—listeners absorb stories differently than they do advice.

Types of Peacemaking Circles

As Circles found various uses, a terminology emerged to distinguish the different types of Circles by their function. This language is still developing and the terms are not universally used, but they are still helpful.

Types of Circles include:

- Talking
- Understanding
- Healing
- Sentencing
- Support
- Community-Building
- Conflict
- Reintegration
- Celebration

Talking Circles—In a Talking Circle, participants explore a particular issue or topic from many different perspectives. Talking Circles do not attempt to reach consensus on the topic. Rather, they allow all voices to be respectfully heard and offer participants diverse perspectives to stimulate their reflections.

Circles of Understanding—A Circle of Understanding is a Talking Circle focused on understanding some aspect of a conflict or difficult situation. A Circle of Understanding is generally not a decision-making Circle; therefore, it does not need to reach consensus. Its purpose is to develop a more complete picture of the context or reason for a particular event or behavior.

Healing Circles—The purpose of a Healing Circle is to share the pain of a person or persons who have experienced trauma or loss. A plan for support beyond the Circle may emerge, but it is not required.

A tenth-grade student was referred to Circle for school attendance issues. In addition, he had also been in trouble for smoking. During the second Circle, he told a story about how he had not felt comfortable in school since being expelled in the fall of his eighth-grade year for the remainder of that year.

No one at the high school had any idea how traumatic the experience was for him until both he and his mother talked about it in the Circle. He told the members that this was the first time since the eighth grade that he felt anyone at school had really tried to understand where he was coming from.[4]

Sentencing Circles—A Sentencing Circle is a community-directed process in partnership with the criminal justice system. It involves all those affected by an offense in deciding an appropriate sentencing plan which addresses the concerns of all participants.

This Circle brings together the person who has been harmed, the person who caused the harm, family and friends of each, other community members, justice system representatives (judge, prosecutor, defense counsel, police, probation officer), and other resource professionals. The participants discuss: 1) what happened, 2) why it happened, 3) what the impact is, and 4) what is needed to repair the harm and prevent it from happening again.

By consensus, the Circle develops the sentence for the person who committed the crime and may also stipulate responsibilities of community members and justice officials as part of the agreement. Preparation for a Sentencing Circle may involve a Healing Circle for the person harmed and a Circle of Understanding for the one who committed the harm before bringing the two parties together.

Support Circles—A Support Circle brings together key people to support a person through a particular difficulty or major change in life. Support Circles often meet regularly over a period of time. By consensus, Support Circles may develop agreements or plans, but they are not necessarily decision-making Circles.

Community-Building Circles—The purpose of a Community-Building Circle is to create bonds and build relationships among a group of people who have a shared interest. Community-Building Circles support effective collective action and mutual responsibility.

Conflict Circles—A Conflict Circle brings together disputing parties to resolve their differences. Resolution takes shape through a consensus agreement.

Reintegration Circles—Reintegration Circles bring together an individual and a group or community from which that individual has been estranged to work toward reconciliation and acceptance of the individual into the group again. Reintegration Circles frequently develop consensus agreements. They have been used for juveniles and adults who are returning to the community from prisons or correctional facilities.

Celebration or Honoring Circles—Celebration Circles bring together a group of people to recognize an individual or a group and to share joy and a sense of accomplishment.

Applications of Peacemaking Circles

Peacemaking Circles have been used for the following:

- Supporting and assisting victims of crime
- Criminal sentencing for juveniles and adults
- Reintegrating inmates into communities upon leaving prison
- Supporting and monitoring chronic offenders on probation
- Providing support for families accused of child abuse and neglect, while keeping the child safe
- Team-building and staff renewal in social service agencies
- Developing mission statements and strategic plans within organizations
- Developing new programs in an agency
- Handling discrimination, harassment, and interpersonal conflicts within the workplace
- Addressing neighborhood disagreements
- Managing classrooms and playground conflicts

- Handling school discipline
- Teaching writing in an alternative school
- Repairing harms inflicted by a sixth-grade class on a substitute teacher
- Processing chemical dependency relapses in a high school for recovering addicts
- Developing education plans for special education students
- Resolving family conflicts
- Grieving losses in a family or community
- Handling environmental and planning disputes
- Facilitating dialogue between immigrant communities and local government
- Facilitating dialogue between rival gangs
- Leading college classes discussions
- Celebrating graduations and birthdays
- Discussing youth presence at a suburban mall

2.
A Circle Story—
Finding a Way to Move Forward after a Worker Strike[4]

In the aftermath of a polarizing state workers' strike, administrators of a juvenile residential facility took a pro-active stance by suggesting that a Circle be called. They hoped this would be a way to get the issues out in the open, allow people to share their stories, create a safe place for feelings to be shared and heard, express what was needed to move on, and to start the healing process.

Our plan was to have a half-day Circle to introduce the process and to set parameters for what could be done to help the agency through this time. This would serve as an opportunity to begin the healing process and to prepare individuals for the second Circle, which would focus more on the emotional issues at the root of the tensions.

A week after this first Circle, we set aside an entire day for a second Circle to deal with the core issues that individuals were struggling with. From the beginning, we acknowledged that these two sessions would likely only be the start of a long process, and that the Circle keepers were neither experts nor problem-solvers, but were present to be support people in guiding the agency through the process.

First Circle

We spent substantial time framing the process and setting the stage for the work we would be doing together. To guide the Circle, we placed the residential program's guiding principles and core values in the center to remind participants of their commitment to help kids. This was important as the team created and voted on these guiding principles and core values, so that they held weight within the work culture. We also asked everyone to imagine a larger circle of students encircling our own, watching the adults model mature problem-solving and serving as a reminder of what is truly important to their purpose of working at this program.

We emphasized and modeled the Circle Process as a safe place to share and hopefully heal, and stressed that this was different than a "staff meeting" or a "mediation session." We did this by working to create a "sacred space" where individuals would be able to listen and speak from the heart, have the right to remain silent, commit to confidentiality, and to respect the talking piece by ensuring that the holder of the piece would be the only person speaking at any one time.

By working to create a sense of ceremony through opening and closing readings/meditations and other rituals, we emphasized the importance of creating a space that was conducive for this type of work. We also emphasized that the group was just as much responsible for co-facilitation as we were as Circle keepers. It was our belief that if we spent significant time and energy introducing the process and setting a tone, we would hopefully nurture an environment in which people would over time become comfortable in being honest with themselves and others.

The first few rounds of the talking piece centered on introductions, "check-ins," and lighthearted questions designed to relax the group and to build some universality among participants. The next round asked Circle members to share what they needed to feel safe through this process. This question was important in order to get people to think in general terms about what they need to feel safe, and also for other Circle members to develop an awareness of how their behavior could potentially impact others.

The next round consisted of an activity in which Circle members were asked to record on an index card how the strike impacted them personally. Individuals were asked to write down if they believed they were harmed by anyone during the strike, and also if they knowingly inflicted harm on anyone. After they finished writing, they were asked to place their index cards in a safe place until we met again, and if they chose to do so, they would then have an opportunity to share their reflections.

This activity was designed so participants would reflect on their personal behavior, as well as explore the impact on self, family, and work relationships that occurred as a result of the strike. We concluded the first Circle by asking participants to share what their hopes were for the residential program and for themselves in the next three months.

Overall, the tone of the first Circle was positive despite the clear tension that existed among participants. It was clear that people wanted to maintain their positive work with kids and valued that above all else. However, there were conflicting views about how to move on after the strike due to deep-seated views on labor unions, individual responses to stress, and current levels of anger. It appeared that some individuals were ready to get into difficult issues right away, while others were very worried about what could happen during the Circle.

Some participants were grateful that a Circle was being held to address the issue, and others claimed not to believe in the process and verbalized their belief that it was a waste of time. Despite the diversity of expectations toward the process, we believed that we were able to set the stage for the following Circle.

Second Circle

After initiating the Circle with an opening reading, we reviewed what we had done in the previous session, emphasizing the program's guiding principles and core values that were at the center of the Circle. Again we asked the group to imagine a larger circle of clients around us that would hopefully keep the group focused on the big picture.

The first pass of the talking piece consisted of a "check-in" where participants were asked to share how they were doing in general terms and also how they felt about returning to the Circle. The next round centered on exploring what was the most stressful thing for individuals and their families during the strike. Both of these rounds took a substantial amount of time as group members spoke eloquently about their experience of stress during the strike, and also about the residual stress as a result of actions that transpired during that time.

The next round gave participants a chance to share their individual impact statements they had written the previous week. This was an emotional round for many as they shared in detail how they believed they were impacted, how they perceived they were harmed, and/or how they believed they may have harmed their co-workers through their actions.

A Circle Story

At the next round we asked the Circle to share what they needed in order to "move on." People shared that they needed a variety of things, including time, patience, understanding, forgiveness, etc. Since many people made apologies during the previous round, we encouraged people to make amends or set plans to address harms during this round.

After doing a good job of articulating what they needed to heal, we transitioned to having Circle participants make commitments about what they as individuals would do to help the program move forward and function in a safe and healthy manner. Again, most people were positive and hopeful and made strong commitments to help the program through this time and to maintain the high quality programming that the facility provides to adolescent boys.

3.
Foundations of Circles

"In every one of us there is a deep desire
to connect to others in a good way."
— Judge Barry Stuart, Yukon, Canada

Values

Peacemaking Circles are not a neutral, value-free process. Rather, they are consciously built on a foundation of shared values. A specific set of values is not prescribed for Circles, but the value framework is the same for all Circles.

Circles assume a universal human wish to be connected to others in a good way. The values of a Circle derive from this basic human impulse. Therefore values that nurture and promote good connections to others are the foundation of the Circle.

There is no single "right" way to express those values, and even though in my experience those values are similar across different groups, they cannot be taken for granted. Peacemaking Circles are intentional and explicit in identifying values before entering dialogue about issues. Because the Circle asks all participants to act on those values within the Circle to the best of their ability, Circle participants must truly claim the values.

Peacemaking Circles: From Crime to Community suggests the following values as foundational for Circles: respect, honesty, humility, sharing, courage, inclusivity, empathy, trust, forgiveness and love.[6] Community Circles of Washington County, Minnesota, identified the following values as the basis of their Circles: respect, humility, compassion, spirituality, and honesty.

Many people believe that young people who get in trouble do not share these values. However, a group of juveniles incarcerated in a correctional facility created a list for their Circle that included respect, openmindedness, responsibility, caring, honesty, and hearing each other's point of view.

These examples illustrate both the common value framework (values that nurture and promote a good connection to others) and the diverse ways that groups may put into words what guides their behavior. When participants consciously choose the values they want to guide their interaction, they are much more deliberate about keeping their behavior aligned with those values. A participant in a pain-filled, gut-wrenching Circle named self-control as the value he wanted to put in the Circle. Later in the Circle he stated, "I'm just glad I put self-control in the Circle because otherwise I wouldn't be using it now."

> Circles assume a universal human wish to be connected to others in a good way.

Ancient teachings

In addition to the values associated with humans being their "best selves," the foundation of the Circle Process includes several assumptions about the nature of the universe. These assumptions are common in the worldview of most indigenous cultures and are often metaphorically associated with the image of the Circle. These assumptions have been passed from generation to generation through cultural teachings.

One of the most important teachings underlying the Circle Process is the assertion that everything in the universe is connected. This teaching tells us that every action affects everything in the universe, that it is impossible to isolate something to act on it without affecting everything else. In this worldview there is no such thing as an objective observer or a detached perspective. Everything is connected.

> **We need the person for whom the Circle is formed just as much as that person needs us.**

A corollary to this assumption is the understanding that we cannot just "get rid of" our problems. An educator, overhearing a group of people talking about restorative justice, exclaimed, "Oh, I get it. Just like 30 years ago when we threw a bottle out the window, we thought we threw it 'away,' and then the environmental movement taught us there is no 'away.' This is the same for people."

When we operate under the illusion that we can throw something away, it comes back to poison us in a way that we may not realize because we have assumed that it is gone. Circles hold at their center the importance of recognizing the impact of our behavior on others and acknowledging the interconnectedness of our fates. Harm to one is harm to all. Good for one is good for all.

Another corollary to this teaching about connection is the assumption that we are interdependent, that we need each other in fundamental ways. A community member in a Circle for a person who committed a crime observed:

What I gotta do to keep what I got is to give it away.
I need to be in Circle. When I'm by myself, it doesn't
go so good. People come together and work together
to try to help each other. Gotta give it away to keep
it. It's just the way it works.

The assumption of the Circle is that we need the person
for whom the Circle is formed just as much as that person
needs us.

Because we all are connected and all are interdependent, each of us has value to the whole. Therefore, Circles
operate from the belief that each person has inherent
dignity and worth. We all equally deserve respect and the
opportunity to voice our perspectives.

This belief that everything is connected, that there is
no objective observer, and that we are profoundly interdependent is now powerfully supported by quantum
physics. Margaret J. Wheatley in her book *Leadership and
the New Science* describes how the shift from a Newtonian
understanding of the universe to a quantum understanding is just now, a century after the key discoveries, being
incorporated into thinking about human relationships and
organizations in Western society.[7]

She writes:

Each of us lives and works in organizations designed
from Newtonian images of the universe. . . Things
can be taken apart, dissected literally or representationally (as we have done with business functions
and academic disciplines), and then put back together
without any significant loss. The assumption is that
by comprehending the workings of each piece, the
whole can be understood. The Newtonian model of

the world is characterized by materialism and reductionism—a focus on things rather than relationships.[8]

In comparison, Wheatley explains the quantum view:

The quantum mechanical view of reality strikes against most of our notions of reality . . . It is a world where *relationship* is the key determiner of what is observed . . . Particles come into being and are observed only in relationship to something else. They do not exist as independent "things." . . . These unseen *connections* between what were previously thought to be separate entities are the fundamental elements of all creation.[9]

Community
Building

Healing

Connections

Circle Keeping
Talking Piece
Guidelines
Ceremony
Consensus

Shared Values

Ancient Teachings

Guidance of Medicine
Wheel Teachings

Perhaps that level of interconnectedness is not familiar to Western cultures, but it is familiar to many indigenous cultures. And thus, ancient wisdom and modern science, coming from two different ways of knowing and vastly different cultures, arrive at the same conclusion. Though modern physics and ancient metaphysics reach the same conclusions, this belief is not at the foundation of many Western social structures that are built on a Newtonian model of objective reality and separable components.

Another ancient teaching foundational for Circles is that human experience has mental, physical, emotional, and spiritual aspects. All of these aspects of human experience are equally important and offer essential gifts to our collective life. Balance among these aspects is important for the health of individuals and communities. Consequently, Circles intentionally create a space in which all of these aspects of human experience are recognized and welcomed.

Emotional and spiritual expressions that reflect the personal perspective of the speaker, but are not assumed to be the same for others, have a place in the Circle. Circles assume that conflicts and difficulties have emotional and spiritual content for participants and that effective resolutions require exploring the emotional and spiritual content as well as the physical and mental content.

Circle Process as practiced in faith-based communities

Thomas W. Porter Jr., Executive Director of JUSTPEACE

Inspired by the work of Kay Pranis, the JUSTPEACE Center for Mediation and Conflict Transformation in the United Methodist Church has found the Circle Process a great gift to the Church. We have found that it:

- Evokes the best of our theology.
- Recognizes the importance of ritual and sacred space and time.
- Emphasizes the significance of relational covenants.
- Encourages deep listening and respectful speaking from the heart.
- Moves us away from parliamentary procedure to consensus decision-making.
- Creates an empowering servant or stewardship understanding of leadership.
- Focuses us on the mission of reconciliation, healing relationships, and creating community.

In short, the Circle Process has helped bring us back to a better and more faithful way of being Church. As the Process gained wide acceptance, we have found that it has the capacity to transform the way we make decisions, the way we conduct our grievance procedures, even the way we experience Holy Communion as the ritual of reconciliation and the healing of relationships.

4.

A Circle Story—
Finding Understanding
in the Classroom[10]

A student in an elementary school threatened to burn down the school following recess. This incident occurred soon after the school shootings in Littleton, Colorado, and his anger sparked fear among his classmates.

The teacher requested a Circle of Understanding for the students, and the next day the entire classroom participated in it. During the Circle, students expressed their feelings about how the threats had impacted them. Many of the students reported experiencing nightmares as a result of the student's threat. The students also reflected on how their own behavior had an effect on the student who made the threat and how they were responsible, to a degree, for his behavior.

At the conclusion of the Circle, the boy agreed to make changes in his own behavior by: 1) not swearing or threatening others, 2) thinking before speaking, and 3) walking away when he was mad to cool down and then talking it out later. He also agreed to write an apology letter to his classmates.

His classmates agreed to make changes in their behavior by: 1) being nicer to him, 2) not telling lies about him, 3) not teasing him, 4) playing with him so he would have more friends, 5) being his partner in class, 6) helping him make new friends, 7) sticking up for him in a good way,

8) forgiving him and giving him a second chance, and 9) playing basketball with him after school.

A previous behavior contract with the boy banned him from the playground for the rest of the school year. His classmates did not want that to happen; instead, they wanted to give him another chance. They felt that if everyone did what he/she agreed to in the Circle, there would be no more problems on the playground. They were right. The boy was given a second chance to play on the playground with his classmates, and he followed through on the conditions of the agreement.

5.
Key Elements of Circles

Structural elements of Circles

Building on the foundation of values and ancient teachings, Circles use five key structural elements to create a safe space for people to connect with others in a good way, even in circumstances of conflict, harm, or difficulty. These elements include ceremony, guidelines, a talking piece, keeping/facilitation, and consensus decision-making.

Ceremony

Opening and closing ceremonies mark the time and space of the Circle as a space apart. It is a distinctly different space because the Circle invites people to be in touch with the value of connecting deeply with others, and it encourages people to drop the ordinary masks and protections that create distance from others.

Opening ceremonies help participants shift gears from the pace and tone of ordinary life to the pace and tone of the Circle. Opening ceremonies help participants to center themselves, be reminded of core values, clear negative energies from unrelated stresses, encourage a sense of optimism, and honor the presence of everyone there.

Closing ceremonies acknowledge the efforts of the Circle, affirm the interconnectedness of those present, convey a sense of hope for the future, and prepare participants to return to the ordinary space of their lives. Opening and

---

closing ceremonies are designed to fit the nature of the particular group and provide opportunities for cultural responsiveness.

Guidelines

The guidelines of the Circle are the commitments or promises that participants make to one another about how they will behave in the Circle. The purpose of the guidelines is to establish clear expectations for conduct based on what the participants need to make the space safe to speak in their authentic voices, and to act from the impulse to be connected to others in a good way. Guidelines are designed to meet the needs of the specific Circle and always include respectful speaking and listening and some form of confidentiality.

> Guidelines are adopted by consensus of the Circle.

The entire Circle, not just the facilitator, is responsible for the creation and implementation of the guidelines. Guidelines are not rigid constraints but supportive reminders of the behavioral expectations of everyone in the Circle. They are not imposed on the participants but rather are adopted by consensus of the Circle.

Developing guidelines begins during the preparation phase and continues when the Circle convenes. If someone disagrees with a proposed guideline, the keeper facilitates a discussion exploring the purpose of the guideline and the concern raised. It is a search for understanding and for common ground to ensure a space that is respectful for all participants.

It is generally not difficult to reach consensus on the guidelines. For example, even in circumstances of hostility, when parties may not value hearing each other, they still want respectful listening as a guideline because *they* wish to be heard respectfully. The guidelines arise out of asking people what they want *for* themselves *from* others and then, naturally, those guidelines apply to everyone in the Circle.

Discussion of guidelines helps Circle participants reflect on how they will be present with one another so they can act more intentionally than they might otherwise, especially in circumstances of conflict or anger.

Talking piece

The talking piece is an object that is passed from person to person around the Circle. As its name implies, the holder of the talking piece has the opportunity to talk while all other participants have the opportunity to listen without thinking about a response. The holder of the talking piece may also choose to offer silence, or the holder may pass the piece without speaking. There is no obligation to speak when the talking piece comes.

The talking piece is a critical element of creating a space in which participants can speak from a deep place of truth. It assures speakers that they will not be interrupted, that they will be able to pause and find the words that express what is on their hearts and minds, that they will be fully and respectfully heard. The talking piece slows the pace of conversation and encourages thoughtful and reflective interactions among participants. It often carries symbolic meaning related to the group's shared values and thus is a concrete reminder to the speaker of those values.

The talking piece creates a level of order in the dialogue that allows the expression of difficult emotions without the process spinning out of control. Because only one person can speak at a time and the talking piece moves in order around the Circle, two people cannot go back and forth at each other when they disagree or are angry. The talking piece spreads the responsibility around the Circle for responding to and managing the difficult feelings. Because Circle participants know the keeper usually will not speak until the talking piece reaches him/her, others in the Circle often respond in mediating ways to expressions of pain, anger, or conflict.

> The talking piece is a critical element of creating a space in which participants can speak from a deep place of truth.

The talking piece is a powerful equalizer. It allows every participant an equal opportunity to speak and carries an implicit assumption that every participant has something important to offer the group. The talking piece facilitates the contributions of quiet people who are unlikely to assert themselves in a typical open dialogue. As it passes physically from hand to hand, the talking piece weaves a connecting thread among the members of the Circle.

Keeping/facilitation

The term "keeper" is commonly used for the facilitator of the Circle. Thomas Porter, director of the United Methodist JUSTPEACE organization, uses the term "steward" when conducting Circles within Christian settings. In this book, I use keeper and facilitator interchangeably. The keeper in a Circle is not responsible for finding solutions or for controlling the group. The keeper's role is to initiate a space that is respectful and safe, and to engage participants in sharing responsibility for the space and for their shared work.

The keeper helps the group access its individual and collective wisdom by opening the space in a careful way and monitoring the quality of the space as the group proceeds. The large role played by the talking piece in regulating the dialogue reduces the role of the keeper as a facilitator relative to other dialogue processes. The keeper may speak without the talking piece but rarely does so.

The role of the keeper is not that of a "neutral," common in Western conflict resolution models. The keeper is a participant in the process and may offer her thoughts, ideas, and stories. Minimizing bias in the facilitator is still a goal of the Circle Process, but this is achieved through caring about everyone in the Circle rather than by holding a clinical distance.

Because guidelines in a Circle are created by consensus of the group and belong to the group, the keeper is not an enforcer but a monitor. If the guidelines are not working, then the keeper draws the attention of the group to the need to address guidelines.[11] Except for small Circles, it is common to have two keepers facilitating a Circle. One of the most important characteristics of an effective keeper is the ability to let go of control, to share responsibility for both the process and the outcomes with the participants of the Circle.

Consensus decision-making

Not all Peacemaking Circles make decisions, but when they do, the decisions are made by consensus. Consensus in the Circle Process is generally understood to mean that all participants are willing to live with the decision and support its implementation.

Consensus decision-making is grounded in a deep commitment to understand the needs and interests of all participants and to work toward meeting all of those needs. It requires deep listening and reflection before making decisions. A commitment to consensus engages participants in helping others meet their needs while also meeting the participant's own needs. Consensus challenges participants to speak truthfully if they cannot live with a decision, and then to help the group find a solution they can live with that meets the needs of the group as well.

Entering a consensus process requires an attitude of exploration rather than of conquering or persuading. The deep and respectful listening to all participants resulting from the use of the talking piece makes consensus decision-making a natural outcome of the Circle Process.

Consensus is not always possible, but it is a rare experience not to reach consensus in a Circle if adequate time is allowed to hear fully all perspectives. When participants feel fully heard and observe that the Circle tried to address their needs, they rarely block consensus, even if they do not get what they wanted in a particular decision.

Consensus gives power to everyone.

If consensus cannot be reached, the decision can revert to whatever process would normally apply. Generally, there will be much richer information available to that process as a result of the Circle.

Consensus decisions produce more effective and sustainable agreements because consensus-based processes give power to everyone. Achieving consensus requires the group to pay attention to the interests of those who are normally powerless. Consensus processes hold the potential for more fundamentally democratic results because all interests must be taken into account. Decisions must ultimately represent everyone involved or consensus will not be achieved. Therefore, decisions must address the interests of everyone to some degree.

Decisions or plans addressing the interests of all participants have a far greater likelihood of success because every participant has something to gain by successful completion of the agreement. Consequently, every participant has an investment in success. Decision-making by consensus generally takes more time in the decision-making process but less time in implementation because of the commitment of all parties to the decision.

These five structural elements—ceremony, guidelines, a talking piece, a keeper, and consensus decision-making constructed on the foundation of shared values and indigenous teachings—create a "container" in which people can draw on the best in themselves to reach out to one another and connect at profound levels.

The importance of storytelling

Storytelling delivers information in a way that opens the listener. When information is asserted or presented cognitively, we immediately engage a screening device to determine whether we agree or disagree. We are primarily engaged mentally and begin thinking about how we will respond.

Storytelling employs a different kind of listening. The body relaxes, settles back, is more open and less anxious. We take in the story before screening the content. We are engaged emotionally as well as mentally. This different kind of listening allows information to be exchanged more thoroughly, leading to much greater understanding between people.

Circles are a storytelling process. They use the history and experience of everyone in the Circle to understand the situation and to look for a good way forward—not through lecturing or giving advice or telling others what to do, but through sharing stories of struggle, pain, joy, despair, and triumph. Personal narratives are the source of insight and wisdom in Circles.

By sharing our individual stories we open places for others to connect to us, to find common ground with us, and to know us more completely. In a respectful speaker/ listener relationship, both individuals open themselves to a deeper connection to the other. When people share stories of pain or mistakes and drop layers of protection, revealing themselves as struggling, vulnerable human beings, we feel more connected to them. It becomes much harder to hold someone as the distant "other" and not feel connected to that person through our common humanity. It becomes more difficult to hold anger or fear or disinterest toward someone who shares pain and vulnerability. Unless we are already familiar with the life history of the speaker, sharing stories of pain and vulnerability usually shatters some assumption we have made about the person telling the story.

> Storytelling strengthens a sense of connectedness, fosters self-reflection, and empowers participants.

Telling our stories is a process of self-reflection. In telling our stories we articulate how we understand what has happened to us, why and how it has impacted us, and how we see ourselves and others. Our way of constructing our stories, which shapes our view of reality, becomes more transparent to us when we speak the story out loud to others.

To feel connected and respected, people need to tell their stories and have others listen. Having others listen to your story is a function of power in our culture. The more power you have, the more people will listen respectfully to your story. To listen respectfully to a person's story is to honor that person's intrinsic worth and to empower the storyteller in a constructive way.

Focusing on relationships

Before trying to work out issues or move to action, the Circle Process must first spend time helping participants connect as human beings. Harold Gatensby, a Tlingit First Nations Circle teacher and mentor from Carcross, Yukon, has applied the Medicine Wheel framework of four equal sections or elements to the Circle Process (see diagram on p. 324.) The teaching of this Medicine Wheel image is that as much time must be spent on getting acquainted and building understanding as is spent on discussing the issues and making action plans.

Getting acquainted at a deeper level and building relationships happens primarily within the Circle itself. The early rounds of the Circle create ways for people to talk about who they are and what is important to them, and to share significant life experiences. These early rounds deliberately do not focus on the issues of contention.

The introduction round often invites people to share something meaningful about themselves. A values round may ask people to name a value they would like to bring to the Circle and why that value is important to them. A storytelling round in a Conflict Circle might invite participants to share an experience in which they had caused harm to another, but then resolved it in a way they felt good about. In these rounds the keepers model the vulnerability of sharing deep feelings. The rounds are posed toward positive sharing.

The Four Relational Elements of Circles
(based on the Medicine Wheel)

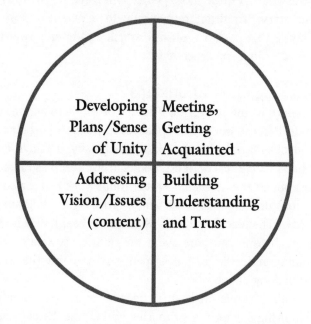

As participants reveal unknown or unseen aspects of themselves from a positive orientation, the negative assumptions others may make about them begin to crack and gradually lose strength. As participants share stories, they discover unexpected ways in which they are alike.

Careful preparation, hospitality when people arrive, a thoughtful opening, collective creation of guidelines, and the use of the talking piece all contribute to creating a space in which people are more likely to risk being vulnerable in the storytelling rounds. Once people are vulnerable with one another, trust begins to build. The level of connectedness and trust directly impacts the effectiveness of the discussion of issues and the development of plans to address the issues.

If a group of people has not developed a sense of connection and trust, discussion of issues often remains at a superficial level. People may not feel safe to speak their deepest truth if they do not have a sense of common ground that comes from knowing others beyond the usual introductions.

There is often a sense of great vulnerability in speaking the truth about difficult issues. Without a sense of trust and connection, people also will not be as quick to offer their gifts or resources that might serve the group's work. Plans that are developed based on a superficial level of information and analysis are ineffective.

A slight, nervous, 20-year-old male sat in the large circle of mostly middle-aged teachers, community members, and criminal justice professionals participating in a training on the Circle Process. The young man had been working with a local Criminal Justice Circle group for nearly a year. He had twice been through treatment for his addictions, particularly to methamphetamines, because of relapses, and recently lost his job because of a positive urine test for drugs. In spite of that, the Circle members who knew him welcomed him warmly with hugs.

As the talking piece came to him in the closing round for the day, he spoke directly and clearly, apologizing to the teachers in the room for the problems he had caused when he was in high school. Looking up from the feather, he spoke with deep conviction, "If it weren't for Circle and for all the caring and support and the wisdom of Circle, I'd be dead. There's so much love and support here. That's way cool. I can feel it right here" (pointing to his heart).[12]

When the plans fail to achieve the desired outcomes, groups typically go back to analyzing the problem and try a new plan. If they still have not built relationships and trust, they still will not get the deeper truth, and the analysis and plan will again fall short of the desired outcomes. Though the relationship-building takes time, it may in the end be more efficient because it supports the creation of effective and sustainable solutions.

Circles use the deep desire to be connected to others in a good way as a platform for developing relationships. That then enables people to probe issues in a more profound way, resulting in more profound resolutions to difficult problems or conflicts.

Stages of Circle Processes

As mentioned earlier, using Peacemaking Circles requires more than arranging chairs in a circle. Circles addressing conflict or harm involve a multi-stage process, and each stage is important for the effectiveness of the process. The four stages in most Circle Processes include determining suitability, preparation, convening the Circle, and follow-up.

Stage 1: Determining suitability. This involves assessing whether the Circle is an appropriate process for this situation by asking these questions:

- Are key parties willing to participate?
- Are trained facilitators available?
- Will the situation allow the time required to use the Circle Process?
- Can physical and emotional safety be maintained?

Stage 2: Preparation

- Identify who needs to participate: Who has been impacted? Who has resources, skills, or knowledge that might be needed? Who has similar life experiences that might add insight?
- Familiarize key parties with the process.
- Begin exploring the context of the issue.

Stage 3: Convening all parties

- Identify shared values and develop guidelines.
- Engage storytelling to build relationships and connections.
- Share concerns and hopes.
- Express feelings.
- Probe underlying causes of conflict or harm.
- Generate ideas for addressing harm or resolving conflict.

- Determine areas of consensus for action.
- Develop agreement and clarify responsibilities.

Stage 4: Follow-up

- Assess progress on agreements. Are all parties fulfilling their obligations?
- Probe for causes of any failure to fulfill an obligation, clarify responsibilities, and identify next steps if the failure continues.
- Adjust agreements as needed based on new information or developments.
- Celebrate successes.

Clearly Stage 3, convening all the parties, will be conducted in a Circle. However, Circles may also be used in the other three stages of the overall process. For example, when a Peacemaking Circle is used for sentencing in a criminal case, the process uses Circles in the steps leading to the actual Sentencing Circle:

• *Stage 1.* The offender may apply to the Circle Process through an Application Circle or Interview Circle.

• *Stage 2.* Preparation may include: a) creation of a support system for the offender, b) creation of a support system for the victim, c) Healing Circle(s) for the victim, d) Circle(s) of Understanding for the offender.

• *Stage 3.* The sentencing process is done in a Circle.

• *Stage 4.* Follow-up Circles may be used at appropriate intervals to review progress on the sentencing agreement.

6.

A Circle Story—
Finding Healing from a Violent Crime[13]

L aughter, hugs, and good-byes filled the air as people milled around the living room of a house in North Minneapolis. An exchange near the doorway of the house told the story of the evening.

"Are you still afraid?" asked a community member.

"No, I will not be afraid again," replied the man in his fifties.

This exchange followed a Peacemaking Circle in which the victim of an armed robbery met with the 17-year-old juvenile who had held a loaded gun to his head in his back yard. In the Circle were the victim's family, a friend, the juvenile's family, numerous community members, and juvenile justice professionals—about 20 people in all. The victim described the trauma of the crime and its impact on his life. The juvenile and his family expressed their regret and concern for the victim. Community members expressed support for both families and a hope that the community can come together to strengthen the neighborhood.

After everyone had a chance to speak, the victim asked to speak again. He looked across the circle of chairs at the juvenile and said, "When you get out of Red Wing (the juvenile correctional facility), I'd like to take you out to lunch."

A short time later, when a break was called in the process, the juvenile approached the victim's son of the same age with an outstretched hand. The son rose from his chair and hugged the juvenile. The juvenile then approached the victim and his wife, who also hugged him. The trauma of the previous six months was transformed into an experience of community support and expressions of remorse for the harm caused to the man and his family.

Before this Circle brought the two families together, separate Circles were held for the victim and the juvenile. The Circle of Understanding for the victim provided an opportunity for the victim to fully express the horror of the experience and its aftermath, including painful remarks by others suggesting that it was no big deal because "nobody got hurt."

Both families felt isolated and alone in their pain before the Circle Process. Neither family felt that the community cared about what was happening to them. Both families expressed surprise at the offers of help and support from community members who had no direct connection to the event. The Circle Process was able to break the cycle of isolation and fear. It gave participants a sense of hope about their future as a community beyond this individual case.

The dialogue of the Circle also brought to the surface important perspectives not often heard. The father and older brother of the juvenile were emphatic in their denunciation of guns. The older brother of the juvenile spoke in eloquent terms about the struggle of growing up as a young black male. Giving voice to these perspectives and raising community and system awareness is an important outcome of the Circle Process.

7.
Organizing a Talking Circle

Sitting in on a Circle is a wonderful way to learn more about the process. If there is no existing Circle available, organizing a Talking Circle is a good place to start. Training and personal healing work are essential before facilitating Circles around interpersonal conflict, trauma, difficult group decisions, or intensely emotional situations. However, it is possible to facilitate a Talking Circle without formal training.

Talking Circles do not attempt to bring a group to consensus or repair serious disruptions in relationships. They simply allow everyone to speak about a particular topic from his or her perspective. Sharing perspectives increases everyone's understanding of the issue and may improve relationships, but a Talking Circle would not attempt to do deep relationship work.

Talking Circles can be used to:

- Check in with one another in an ongoing group (class, staff, civic organization, committee, advisory board, project group).
- Reflect on a group experience such as a movie, video, speaker, or book.
- Give feedback to a leader or facilitator of a group process.

- Provide input to decision makers.
- Dialogue about community or social concerns such as racism.
- Explore different meanings of an experience or event for people.
- Share intergenerational perspectives.
- Exchange divergent points of view on an emotional topic such as gay marriage or abortion.

The following section will describe how to organize a Talking Circle around a community concern. The community could be a workplace, school, church, or neighborhood.

Begin by choosing a topic for the Circle. The topic should be something of keen interest for you as the organizer. Frame a statement of intent for the Talking Circle: What is the purpose of the Talking Circle? Then work through the four stages of the Circle Process as follows.

Stage 1: Suitability

Assess the suitability of the Talking Circle Process for the identified purpose by answering the following questions:

- Are there people who are willing to participate—does the topic matter to anyone? If not, then a Circle is *not* appropriate.
- Am I (the organizer) hoping to convince others of a particular point of view or change others? If the answer is yes, the Circle is *not* the appropriate forum.
- Am I open to hearing and respecting perspectives very different from mine? If not, then a Circle is *not* appropriate.
- Is the intent respectful of all possible participants? If not, then a Circle is *not* appropriate.

Stage 2: Preparation

After determining that a Talking Circle is a suitable forum for the dialogue you are interested in, begin preparations:

- Identify possible participants, making sure to include people with a variety of perspectives. The potential benefit of a Circle is dramatically reduced if all participants already view the topic the same way. The participants may be an existing group.
- Determine who will keep (facilitate) the Circle. If you are planning to be the keeper, recruit someone who will support you in the responsibility of maintaining a safe space for respectful dialogue.
- Choose a time and place for the Talking Circle, keeping in mind the importance of warmth, hospitality, and access. Make sure the space allows for a sufficient number of chairs to be arranged in a circle with no furniture inside the circle.
- Extend invitations to possible participants with an explanation of the topic, the purpose of the Circle, and the nature of the process.
- Choose a talking piece that will have meaning to the group and will encourage respectful speaking and listening.
- Plan an opening ceremony to set the tone of the relationship space of the Circle (e.g. a reading, deep breathing, music). In planning this and the centerpiece below, make sure that you do not choose something that may be misunderstood or alienating to participants.
- Decide whether you wish to create a centerpiece for the Circle, such as a cloth with a candle or flowers, or other objects that have meaning related to the group or the topic.

- Decide whether you will have food at the Circle and make the necessary arrangements. (Food can be shared at the beginning or end of a Circle.)
- Draft questions that will help participants get acquainted and engage the topic of dialogue.
- Spend time reflecting or meditating on your intention and the importance of entering the Circle with openness and acceptance of others.

Stage 3: Convening

Having made the preparations, arrive early at the space. Make sure the physical set-up is appropriate. Set up the centerpiece if you have one planned. Take some time to breathe deeply and clear your mind of distractions. Follow these steps to convene the Circle:

- Greet participants as they arrive.
- When everyone is present and it is time to start, invite everyone to take a seat.
- Welcome everyone and thank them for coming.
- Conduct the opening ceremony.
- Share again the purpose of the Talking Circle and your intent.
- Introduce the talking piece and explain how it functions. Explain that the talking piece will be passed around the Circle, allowing everyone an opportunity to speak. Only the person holding the talking piece may speak. The only exception is that the keeper (facilitator) may speak without the talking piece if it is necessary for healthy functioning of the Circle. Emphasize that one can choose not to speak by passing the talking piece or holding it in silence.
- Develop guidelines. Describe the importance of the Circle as a place where people can speak their truth.

Pass the talking piece in order around the Circle and ask participants to identify promises they would like from the other participants for making the Circle a place where they can speak the truth.

Record the suggested guidelines on a flip chart or notepad. At the end of the round, read the list to the group. Ask the participants whether they can commit to those guidelines for their process. Pass the talking piece again for individual responses. If there is not consensus, seek modifications that everyone can accept.

- If there are time parameters for the Circle, explain those and ask participants to keep those in mind and to take responsibility for making sure that everyone has adequate opportunity to speak.

- Using the talking piece, initiate a round of introductions even if the participants already know one another. Pose a question for participants to answer in addition to saying who they are. This question is intended to help participants know more about each other before beginning the topic discussion.

  You might ask how the participants are connected to the organizer, or what life experience brought them to be interested in the topic, or what experience they have had with dialogue about difficult or controversial subjects. One purpose of this question is to help participants see commonalities even though they may have very different opinions on the topic. The keeper speaks first in this round and models the kind of sharing that is invited from the participants.

- Begin the dialogue about the chosen topic with a question inviting participants to share their thoughts and feelings about the issue. Pose the question for the group and pass the talking piece for responses. In this round it is usually good for the keeper to speak last.

- Pass the talking piece again for people to respond to what they have heard from others in the previous round.
- If there is time for additional passes of the talking piece, follow the major threads of dialogue that emerged in the earlier rounds.
- If people are interrupting, speaking without the talking piece, or are disrespectful in any way, suspend the dialogue about the issue and revisit the guidelines, asking participants if they can recommit to those guidelines or if any changes are needed.
- About 15 minutes before the ending time of the Circle, pass the talking piece again, asking participants for their feelings about the experience of the Circle or any closing comments they wish to make.
- Offer closing remarks that summarize the experience from your perspective, relate to the original intent, identify what you learned, and honor the achievement of the group in creating and maintaining respectful space. Thank everyone for participating and committing to a respectful process.
- Conduct a closing ceremony that marks the end of the process, reminds people of their interconnectedness, and emphasizes positive potential (e.g. a reading, music, silent reflection).

Stage 4: Follow-up

Follow-up is critical for many kinds of Circles, but a Talking Circle does not generally require follow-up unless the group decides to continue its dialogue or take some further steps. As a keeper, you may wish to seek feedback from participants about what worked and what didn't in the process. Personal reflection on your role as a keeper and debriefing with your co-keeper or support person is always important following a Circle.

These steps are provided as a general guide. Circles are not rigid, but certain elements such as opening and closing ceremonies, use of the talking piece, and the creation of guidelines are essential. With minor modifications, the same steps are used for other types of Talking Circles. For example, the preparation stage for organizing a Check-In Circle or a Circle to reflect on a shared experience (e.g. in a classroom) is simpler, because the topic, participants, and place and time of the Circle are typically already determined.

8.
A Circle Story—
Finding Respect
across Generations[14]

Two neighborhood organizations in Milwaukee became interested in restorative justice and began dialogue with David, a local prosecutor who has been very active in developing restorative practices in the city. They organized a short information session on Circles and remained in dialogue over a period of time, exploring ways to use a restorative approach to break the isolation experienced by many elderly and youth. That isolation breeds fear and mistrust, diminishing the quality of life, especially for seniors.

Barbara and Jeanne, the organizers, decided to hold a Talking Circle involving seniors and young people to assess the level of interest in using Peacemaking Circles in the future to address issues of isolation and personal safety for seniors and youth. They wanted to determine if there was enough interest in the process to justify investing in training for Peacemaking Circles.

In preparation they identified seniors to invite to the Circle. They chose seniors who had expressed both fear and a desire for a better relationship with youth. They worked in partnership with the local Boys and Girls Club and identified a leadership group of teens from the club program to invite to the Circle.

The invitations went to 22 seniors and 10 youth. The demographics of this neighborhood have changed dramatically over the years. The seniors were mostly white, the youth a mixture of African American, Hispanic, and white. The organizers asked David, the prosecutor, to keep the Circle because he is an experienced keeper. They chose the space (a room at the Boys and Girls Club) and time (3:30 to 5:00 p.m.) for the Circle and planned the food. They produced and distributed the invitation. They also planned the opening activity, which involved making masks for Mardi Gras.

In preparation, David as keeper chose the centerpiece and the talking piece for the Circle. In consultation with the organizers, David crafted the questions to use in the Circle.

The organizers arrived early to set up the food and the art materials for making masks. David set up the circle of chairs and the centerpiece, a wood carving of intertwined figures. He also took some quiet time to center himself and focus on deep breathing.

As people arrived for the Circle, they were greeted warmly and invited to make Mardi Gras masks with the art materials. Twelve of the invited seniors and 10 of the youth came to the Circle.

When the group convened in the circle of chairs, the organizers opened with remarks about Mardi Gras and the meaning of the masks. David introduced the talking piece, a beaded feather, and described the significance of the feather which had been given to him by colleagues after they attended a Circle training. David also described how the talking piece is used, emphasizing the importance of respectful speaking and listening.

Using the talking piece, David then invited participants to share their names and talk about how long they had lived in the neighborhood or had been coming to the Boys and Girls Club. One participant said that she had lived in the same house for 65 years, and she spoke at length about her history in the neighborhood.

For the second round of the talking piece, David invited people to share a story of something that makes them proud to live in this neighborhood or to be part of the Boys and Girls Club.

The third and final round of the talking piece offered participants the opportunity to share something they learned that day. One of the youth responded, "I learned that old people can be really cool." An older adult reflected that she learned it didn't matter what age you are or what race you are, you could still listen to one another.

At closing the participants stood and did a "penguin clap" by holding their arms slightly out from their sides so that their hands overlapped with the next person, and then clapped their hand against the hand of their neighbor on each side in the Circle. The "penguin clap" suggests connectedness without imposing intimacy and is very playful.

At the close of the Circle, two girls, who at times seemed not to be paying attention, went immediately up to some seniors and began talking with them. The girls expressed eagerness to do it again. The driver who transported the seniors home reported that they were thrilled with the experience and were very happy that they had participated. The group plans to do more work bringing seniors and youth together.

9.
Circles in Perspective

*"This is terribly counter-cultural because we want quick
fixes. We are all starving for community. It's a wonderful place
to go and say something and know you'll be heard. It gives us
another way than just dividing people into us and them."*
— Community Circle participant

Community-building impact

Storytelling is critical to the creation of community, connection, and collective action. And quantum physics
tells us that it is not the content of matter which defines it
but its relationships to other pieces of matter.

The process of weaving also provides a useful metaphor
for building community. Relationships are like the threads
in the fabric of a community, and the shared values of the
culture and community create the framework, or loom, for
weaving the relationships together.

As the spinning wheel is a tool for creating the threads,
so is storytelling a tool for creating relationships. And as
the shuttle weaves the threads into a fabric, the relationships woven together form community.

One of the most important contributions of Circles is
the strengthened web of relationships among a group of
people. It may be in a classroom, neighborhood, workplace, family, or faith group. As people sit together, talk
about values, share personal stories, and work through

disagreements in an atmosphere of respect and caring, they weave strong cords of connection among themselves. Those connections increase the community's capacity to take care of all its members and to find solutions when problems arise.

Circles offer the opportunity for members of a community to converse about what they expect from each other and what they are willing to commit to in terms of standards of behavior. In Circles they can build those standards of behavior from shared values and an understanding of how their choices impact others.

How is a Circle different from other similar processes?

There are a variety of processes that look similar to Peacemaking Circles and share key characteristics. Because of the similarities, some people assume that Circles are the same as these processes. Circles differ from these processes in significant ways that affect relationships and outcomes.

Circles and groups

Staff in a juvenile correctional facility, upon learning about Peacemaking Circles, suggested that the groups they

> "What do you do here?" a woman asked, noting that the atmosphere around the building had changed. "There were always lots of kids hanging around, making a lot of noise and they never helped open the door when my arms were loaded. Now it's quieter and when they are around, they run to open the door for me."
>
> The woman she was addressing had led several Circles with neighborhood kids and it had apparently changed the climate of the neighborhood.[15]

do with youth are the same as Circles. In a subsequent training with youth in that facility, the youth were asked if the Circle was the same as their groups. They answered with an emphatic "NO." The youth identified power considerations as a key difference.

In their groups, the facilitator is judging and evaluating their behavior and level of participation. The facilitator has specific expectations about what the youth should say or not say. Under those circumstances, the youth frequently do not feel safe to speak their truth. If one person in a group has power over others and can use what happens in the group in an evaluative process without consensus of the group, then it is not a Peacemaking Circle. The youth were very aware that in group they are not all equal, which is a core prerequisite of Circles.

Circles and therapy

In a Peacemaking Circle, clinical or professional expertise is not the primary resource for gaining insight or for understanding issues. Storytelling by the participants, based on their personal narratives, and self reflection are the main sources of insight.

Additionally, unlike in most therapy, the keeper in a Circle is a participant and may share life experiences that are relevant to the Circle dialogue. A therapist may be a participant in a Circle and share clinical expertise as part of the information the Circle considers, but the therapist would not be responsible for managing all the dynamics of the Circle as they typically might in a therapy role. The Circle facilitator does not direct or manage the work of the group. In a Circle, participants are not only responsible for their own behavior but they share responsibility for the quality of the space of the group as a whole.

Circles and classroom meetings

Many classroom management books and social skills curricula, particularly on the elementary and middle-school level, encourage using the class meeting. The class meeting is a time when students learn and practice social skills such as giving and receiving compliments, listening, empathy, problem-solving, conflict resolution, anger management and identification, and expression of feelings.

These skills are taught through games or activities, often while the students are sitting in a circle. However, key Circle elements may be missing from these activities, such as the use of the talking piece, permission to pass, and the clear expectation that the piece will go around the circle in order.

Challenges

The Circle Process is based on a simple notion: Because we all want to be in good relationships with others, when we create a space that is respectful and reflective, people can find their way through anger, pain, and fear to find common ground and take care of one another. Though the concept is simple, the practice is not.

In many ways our culture encourages separation, demonization of those who disagree, competition, hierarchy, and reliance on experts to solve problems. These tendencies in our collective life create a powerful momentum in a direction opposite that of Circles.

Circles are raising very difficult questions of meaning and personal commitment in the context of community life: What does spirituality mean in a public process? How do we honor one another's spiritual expression? What symbols are meaningful in a diverse culture? How do we invest meaning in symbols and keep that meaning fresh and vibrant? What is the responsibility of the individual to the larger whole? What are our fundamental assumptions about human nature? What does "speaking from the heart" require of us? Can we keep our hearts open when something hurts us? Can we truly live these values?

Common struggles are apparent in various Circle groups. It is very challenging to shift from giving advice and providing answers to sharing personal stories and raising genuine questions (ones to which you do not already have the answer). Most Circles struggle to find that tone which recognizes that we are all inseparable parts of a whole.

Circles raise difficult questions of meaning and personal commitment in the context of community life.

Many Circles are also struggling with the relationship between the lay members and system professionals who sit in Circle. The new roles for professionals are not clear. We tell them to leave their title at the door, but it is not that simple in practice. Professionals have information that is useful to the Circle and they have responsibilities that do not end when they are in Circle.

The interface between the Circle Process and social institutions is very sensitive. The Circle seeks truth and aims to create a space in which participants feel safe to speak their truth knowing that, though they must be accountable for their actions, they will not be disrespected or deliberately harmed. If information revealed in Circle triggers an adversarial process, the resulting actions may betray the Circle's commitment to honor the dignity and voice of every person.

Mandatory reporting creates a dilemma—not because the information should be kept secret but because the information may be revealed in an atmosphere that promises respectful treatment even for those who have made mistakes. Yet the Circle cannot guarantee respectful, non-harming treatment once the information is reported to an adversarial system.

Issues of confidentiality are very thorny in practice. It is critical to elicit truth in order to resolve problems, but there is enormous responsibility to make sure that truth-telling does not put people in jeopardy of harm to their essential being.

Because decisions in Circle are made by consensus, pressure may be put on someone who does not agree to simply go along. This pressure may be felt even if nothing is said. People who have not experienced power or voice in their lives may assume that they had better go along with the rest of the group whether they agree or not. It takes consistent and repeated effort to convey to all participants that their truth and perspective is welcomed, even when it means that the process is prolonged because consensus has not been reached.

For advocates of Circles, it is a challenge to refrain from making judgments about people who erect barriers to Circles or who work against the vision of Circles. The Circle asks us to remain open to everyone and to honor the inherent dignity of everyone—even when that person may not be honoring the inherent dignity of someone else or the values we hold dear in Circle. The power of the vision sometimes evokes a passion that blunts the ability to deeply hear voices that disagree.

Even when Circles do not reach the full flow of human heart and spirit, they are usually powerful. Several weeks after a widely criticized circle case, the judge reflected, "There were faults. This didn't work perfectly. But as I sit here and think about it, this worked as well as any case in court."

10.
A Circle Story—
Finding Connection within Family[16]

For the holidays this year, my nieces and nephews, who normally exchange gifts, decided instead to donate their gift money to a charity—a rather huge step for a bunch of teenagers and college kids. The kids ended up donating over a hundred dollars to an organization for battered women and children. They had no expectations of gifts at our extended family gathering. Just being together was what mattered most to them.

We gathered for our extended family holiday celebration, as usual, on New Year's Eve: four of my brothers, two sisters, and all of our kids for a grand total of 22 individuals. After presenting my mother—"Grandma"—with a new table-top keyboard, a few gifts managed to find their way into the room. Boxes of candy were presented by some, baskets or books from another. Tape measures for all of the guys from the carpenter. I, on the other hand, thought we had agreed to no gifts and stuck to it. I sat there, watching those who just couldn't let gifts "go," and at that moment decided to give them a gift of my own.

Grandma finished her rendition of "The Entertainer" on her new keyboard, and I asked the family to be seated so I could present my gift to them. We were already in somewhat of a circle, so the space was set. I shared with my brothers, sisters, mother, and all of our kids what the staff at Minnesota Correctional Facility Initiative in Moose Lake have been attempting with the Conflict Resolution Initiative: to improve communication, build relationship, and change culture.

I explained a Circle and its intent, and asked permission to share this "gift of communication" with them. Rather timidly my family agreed. I chose for a talking piece a basket that I had just received and suggested that when they see that basket at the cabin, they think of all of the things we shared in this Circle during the holidays.

My question to my family was, "What in the past year has touched you?" and "What do you look forward to in the next year?" The honesty of emotions presented and the depth to which they went surprised even me. A death in the family, loneliness at college, elation over a scholarship, the loss of a job, service in Iraq, thankfulness for a promotion, and many more memories from the past year were shared. Hopes for the future included looking forward to being with family, vacations, being with cousins, and having loved ones home from service.

I reluctantly ended the Circle after three passes of the talking piece, but further discussion of the content went on throughout the evening. Family members tearfully thanked me for this "gift" and look forward to doing it again.

Keeping in touch—communicating—through good and bad is vital to all of us, no matter where we work, but it is especially vital to family.

11.
Conclusion

"Circles take the hard things and bring out the beauty."
— Circle participant

I offer this book with the recognition that it describes my own understanding of Circles. Although many wonderful mentors have shaped my understanding, any particular point of view is limited because it is the view of one point on the rim of the Circle. I can only know my truth. I cannot know the truth for others.

I am deeply grateful for the teachers who brought Circles into my life and for the hundreds and hundreds of people who have shared with me in Circle profound stories of personal struggles. In Circle, through the stories of others and in sharing my own story, I have learned more about who I am and have found my place in community. And in the marvelously paradoxical nature of Circles, while finding my place I also found greater humility—a greater awareness of the limitations of my place.

Peacemaking Circles provide a way to bring people together to hold difficult conversations and to work through conflict or differences. The Circle Process is a way of getting the most complete picture people can of themselves, of one another, and of the issues at hand to enable them to move together in a good way. Circles are based on an assumption of positive potential: that something good can always come out of whatever situation we are in. Circles also assume that no one of us has the whole picture, that it is only by sharing all of our perspectives that we can come closer to a complete picture. Sharing individual perspectives and wisdom creates a collective wisdom much greater than the sum of the parts.

I believe that the Circle is a pathway for bringing together ancient wisdom of communal life with modern wisdom about individual gifts and the value of dissent and difference. In a Circle we honor each individual *and* we honor the collective. In a Circle we reach deep within ourselves *and* we reach outward to connect to the community of the Circle.

Modern Western societies struggle with a lack of connection and with a failure to recognize their interrelatedness. On the other hand, many highly communal societies struggle to make space for different voices and perspectives. In our wonderfully complex, multi-cultural society, those two worldviews are living side by side and have the opportunity to learn directly from each other. The Circle is a crucible for that learning. In the Circle we can find a healthy balance between individual and group needs.

I believe that the Circle is also a pathway for healing past harms as a society. Shame and the fear of losing love or respect are enormous barriers to facing harm we have caused.

When whole societies or groups of people need to acknowledge harm, it is even more difficult. In a Circle we acknowledge our mistakes *and* we hold ourselves and each other in compassion. We are never alone in a Circle. That compassion and the connection we feel to others create an environment in which we can face the painful reality of our impact on others. From acknowledgment can begin the healing process for ourselves and for those who were harmed.

Conclusion

We have only begun to scratch the surface of ways in which the Circle Process can change the content and meaning of our lives. We are limited only by our imaginations, our willingness to be in respectful and loving relationship with every part of creation, and our ability to allow the pattern of the Circle to emerge without trying to manage or control it.

My understanding of Circles continues to evolve. I share my thoughts about Circles not as absolutes, but as part of a continuing dialogue and journey of learning. And I am grateful for the interest and gifts others bring to this exploration of our human capacity for connection and reflection.

The Same

> This is a time when
> Doing
> is split off from
> Knowing,
> and Being
> is
> hardly at all.
>
> But here and there
> on this side of the horizon,
> people meet in sacred circles
> to form communities
> and speak their hearts
> that seek the same.[18]
>
> — Meir Carasso

Appendix:
The Circle Process in Schools
Cynthia Zwicky, M.Ed., Minneapolis Public Schools

The Circle Process and schools are a natural fit. There are many ways that the Circle has been incorporated into the fabric of the Minneapolis Public Schools.

Circles for conflict resolution

Schools are a place where teaching and learning occur naturally. Sometimes this occurs through lessons planned and taught by a teacher, but it can also occur at the hands or words of a peer. Schools are a place where conflict is a daily occurrence as well. Therefore, they provide the perfect setting for teaching and learning about conflict resolution, and the Circle becomes an essential tool for the lesson.

In one third-grade classroom, a teacher had been using the Circle for a variety of purposes. Having become acquainted with the Circle Process, several girls in this class who were struggling with following school rules and staying out of trouble got together on their own during recess to hold a daily Circle. The purpose of the Circle was to support one another to stay on the right path. They set goals for themselves and used this Circle time to check in on their personal progress.

The Circle is, by design, inclusive and equal. Because of this, it can become a place where anyone participating helps find the solution. One example is from a multi-aged classroom of six- to nine-year-olds. On the playground, one boy had knocked down a girl classmate and lain on top of her. This left her shaken, and friends on the playground came to comfort her.

That afternoon, during the classroom Circle, she acknowledged her friends for helping her when she was scared. Curious, another student asked why she was scared, and she explained what happened. The teacher confessed to the group that she did not know how to respond. Then she opened it up for them to respond. As the Circle proceeded, the students began to find the solution.

Finally one student confronted the boy, "Why did you do that to her?" He responded, in a subdued voice, "Because I like her." The response came from the students, "Then why don't you do something so she likes you back?"

The teacher knows that she would not have been able to come up with that solution. It was through the power of the Circle, and collective responsibility, that the issue was resolved.

Community-building Circles

At the beginning of the school year, every teacher gets her/his class list and anticipates the arrival of the new students. As the year begins, Circles are often used to build community. Developing a healthy classroom community creates a foundation for conflict resolution.

We *learn* to be in community—it doesn't always happen by virtue of being in the same place at the same time. Students who have benefited from the use of a daily Circle in their classroom noticed a difference from previous years. "I know everyone's name in my class this year, and I didn't last year," said a sixth grader. The Circle provides everyone the opportunity to speak and to be heard. In this way, we can be assured that no one gets left out.

Perhaps equally important and often overlooked is the importance of building community among adults. Relational trust between teachers is an important factor in student achievement. In one school, it was the teachers who first sat in Circle together at the beginning of the school year and then used it in their classrooms with their students.

They noted the positive effects immediately in the same way their students did. One commented, "We've been working together for four years, and I never knew your son went to the same school as my daughter!" Learning first-hand how beneficial the Circle could be to building community has provided a strong impetus for teachers to begin practicing it in their own classrooms.

Circles as a part of the curriculum

Teachers have also used the Circle as a place to teach a lesson. In a seventh-grade social studies class, the teacher had the students discuss their reactions to the movie *Roots* while they sat in Circle as an alternative to filling out a worksheet. The interactive forum provided the students the opportunity to go deeper into the meaning and their personal feelings around this difficult and complex movie.

Because Circles are a place where the person as an individual is valued, it becomes a safe place to learn and discuss opinions expressed from the heart. It benefits the teachers because they are able to hear every student's voice, something that is not always possible during a whole-class discussion.

The Circle can also be used to strengthen existing curricula. Numerous social skills and anti-bullying curricula encourage students to speak up when they are being teased. Teaching these strategies in the Circle can also provide students with an ideal forum for speaking out. With an established protocol for using the Circle in one's classroom, students will be more likely to try some of the new strategies and coping skills identified in many of these curricula.

The Circle can also be a place where students learn from each other's challenges and successes. A middle school student who had used the Circle reports, "I like [using the Circle] because if someone is having the same problem as you are, you can listen and hear how they solved it."

Conclusion

The uses for Circles in school settings are infinite and are by no means limited to the ones described here. In preparing future generations for this world, the Circle becomes an essential tool for imparting knowledge, providing a forum for reflective dialogue, and encouraging the use of creative and peaceful solutions to conflict. The possibilities are endless.

Endnotes

1 From "Soul Food," *The Well* no. 7 (March 2002). This is hte online newsletter of the Church Council on Justice and Corrections, Ottawa, Canada. See www.ccjc.ca.

2 For more information about Circles, see Pranis, Stuart, and Wedge.

3 For an overview of restorative justice, see Howard Zehr.

4 From a report on In-School Behavior Intervention Grants. See www.education.state.mn.us.

5 Matt Johnson wrote this description of a Circle Process he facilitated with Paula Schaefer while working for AMICUS, a non-profit organization working wiht prison inmates and parolees in Minneapolis, MN.

6 See Pranis, Stuart, and Wedge.

7 (San Francisco: Berrett-Koehler Publishers, 1992.)

8 Ibid., pp. 6, 8-9

9 Ibid., pp. 9-10

10 From a Minnesota Department of Education report on In-School Behavior Intervention Grants. See www.education.state.mn.us.

11 The how-to's of monitoring versus enforcing are subtle skills that require specific training and more explanation than can be provided in a book of this length.

12 Story provided by the author.

13 Ibid.

14 Ibid.

15 Ibid.

16 By Cindy Zetah, "The Gift of Circle," *CRI Newsletter* (February 2004), p. 3.

Suggested Reading

Baldwin, Christina. *Calling the Circle: The First and Future Culture* (Newberg, OR: Swan-Raven, 1994; reprint, New York: Bantam Doubleday Dell, 1998).

Bolen, Jean Shinoda. *The Millionth Circle—How to Change Ourselves and the World: The Essential Guide to Women's Circles* (Berkeley: Conari Press, 1999).

Bopp, Judie, et al., *The Sacred Tree: Reflections on Native American Spirituality* (Lethbridge, Alberta: Four Worlds International Institute,1984).

Boyes-Watson, Carolyn. *Peacemaking Circles and Urban Youth: Bringing Justice Home* (St Paul, MN: Living Justice Press, 2008).

Engel, Beverly. *Women Circling the Earth: A Guide to Fostering Community, Healing, and Empowerment* (Deerfield Beach, FL: Health Communications, 2000).

Garfield, Charles, Cindy Spring, and Sedonia Cahill. *Wisdom Circles: A Guide to Self-Discovery and Community Building in Small Groups* (New York: Hyperion, 1998).

Pranis, Kay, Barry Stuart, and Mark Wedge. *Peacemaking Circles: From Crime to Community* (St. Paul: Living Justice Press, 2003). See www.livingjusticepress.org.

Ross, Rupert. *Returning to the Teachings: Exploring Aboriginal Justice* (Toronto: Penguin Books Canada, 1996).

Wheatley, Margaret J. *Leadership and the New Science* (San Francisco: Berrett-Koehler Publishers, 1992).

Zehr, Howard. *The Little Book of Restorative Justice* (Intercourse, PA: Good Books, 2002).

Zimmerman, Jack, with Virginia Coyle. *The Way of Council* (Las Vegas: Bramble Books, 1996).

About the Author

Kay Pranis is a trainer and writer on Peacemaking Circles and restorative justice. She served as the Restorative Justice Planner for the Minnesota Department of Corrections from 1994 to 2003.

Since 1998, Kay has conducted Circle trainings in a diverse range of communities—from schools to prisons to workplaces to churches, and from rural towns in Minnesota to Chicago's South Side to Montgomery, Alabama. She has written numerous articles on restorative justice and co-wrote *Peacemaking Circles: From Crime to Community, Doing Democracy with Circles: Engaging Communities in Public Planning, Heart of Hope: A Guide for Using Peacemaking Circles to Develop Emotional Literacy, Promote Healing & Build Healthy Relationships* and *Circle Forward: Building A Restorative School Community.*

Kay's intention in her work is to create spaces in which people can be in more loving connection with each other. Kay's experience as a parent and a community activist form the foundation of her vision for peacemaking and community-building.

She is available for Circle trainings and can be reached at kaypranis@msn.com or at 651/698-9181.

Group Discounts for
The Big Book of Restorative Justice
ORDER FORM

If you would like to order multiple copies of *The Big Book of Restorative Justice* for groups you know or are a part of, please email **bookorders@skyhorsepublishing.com** or fax order to **(212) 643-6819**. (Discounts apply only for more than one copy.)

Photocopy this page and the next as often as you like.

The following discounts apply:

1 copy	$14.99
2-5 copies	$13.49 each (a 10% discount)
6-10 copies	$12.74 each (a 15% discount)
11-20 copies	$11.99 each (a 20% discount)
21-99 copies	$10.49 each (a 30% discount)
100 or more	$8.99 each (a 40% discount)

Free Shipping for orders of 100 or more!

Prices subject to change.

Quantity   Price   Total

_____ copies of **Big Book** of **Restorative Justice** @ _____ _____

(Standard ground shipping costs will be added for orders of less than 100 copies.)

METHOD OF PAYMENT

❐   Check or Money Order
       *(payable to **Skyhorse Publishing** in U.S. funds)*

❐   Please charge my:
❐ MasterCard ❐ Visa
❐ Discover   ❐ American Express
#_____

Exp. date and sec. code_____

Signature _____

Name _____

Address _____

City_____

State _____

Zip_____

Phone _____

Email _____

SHIP TO: (if different)
Name _____

Address _____

City_____

State _____

Zip_____

Call: (212) 643-6816
Fax: (212) 643-6819
Email: bookorders@skyhorsepublishing.com
(do not email credit card info)